BEYOND
DIGITAL

BEYOND DIGITAL

How Great Leaders
Transform Their Organizations
and Shape the Future

Paul Leinwand
Mahadeva Matt Mani

HARVARD BUSINESS REVIEW PRESS
Boston, Massachusetts

HBR Press Quantity Sales Discounts

Harvard Business Review Press titles are available at significant quantity discounts when purchased in bulk for client gifts, sales promotions, and premiums. Special editions, including books with corporate logos, customized covers, and letters from the company or CEO printed in the front matter, as well as excerpts of existing books, can also be created in large quantities for special needs.

For details and discount information for both print and ebook formats, contact booksales@harvardbusiness.org, tel. 800-988-0886, or www.hbr.org/bulksales.

The web addresses referenced in this book were live and correct at the time of the book's publication but may be subject to change.

Cataloging-in-Publication data is forthcoming.

ISBN: 978-1-64782-232-3
eISBN: 978-1-64782-233-0

The paper used in this publication meets the requirements of the American National Standard for Permanence of Paper for Publications and Documents in Libraries and Archives Z39.48-1992.

To all those who inspired us to keep learning

Contents

BEYOND
DIGITAL

1

Shape Your Future

The future cannot be predicted, but futures can be invented.

—Dennis Gabor, Nobel prize–winning physicist

The digital age began almost 75 years ago, with the invention of the transistor. The internet is more than 50 years old. The IBM PC was introduced 40 years ago. Even companies that we think of as digital pioneers are aging: Apple is 45 years old, and Google is coming up on 25. Since the first commercial internet browser was created (going on 30 years ago), "being digital" has become a business mantra. But that is no longer enough. We must now focus on building new forms of advantage rather than just digitizing what we have done in the past.

Yes, the underpinnings of business today are digital, but digitization has become a long road to equivalency, and an expensive one at that. Creating sustainable advantage requires more than digitization. It requires understanding that the nature of competitive advantage has shifted—and that being digital is not enough.

It's time to move beyond digital.

Retail shows why. As in most industries, companies took retail digital starting in the second half of the 1990s. Going digital created

1

great efficiencies in managing inventory, sped up the processing of transactions, and allowed for analytics that supported buying and distribution. These changes meant lowered prices and generally improved customer experience—but they didn't fundamentally change the process of retail. Companies still focused largely on having (and growing) their retail footprint, buying inventory they believed their customers wanted, often over-bought non-staples, and discounted what didn't sell. They just reduced the quantities involved and made their mistakes faster.

Now look at Best Buy (a big-box electronics retailer based in the United States), which didn't just digitize its operations in the face of fierce price competition from online retailers. It set out to do something much bolder—going beyond selling electronics to help consumers address the significant challenges they had with everything that followed the moment of purchase. It built the Geek Squad to provide customers both in-home and in-store technical support and service, and leveraged many digital advances to accomplish that task. As a result, Best Buy builds deeper relationships with customers, offers technical help, learns about customer habits and wants, and helps customers realize the full value of their investments in electronics and technology. Best Buy didn't just digitize what it had been previously doing but reimagined its role in the world and how digital could help it fulfill that role. As a result, it has thrived even as so many big-box retailers have been shuttering stores.

In the world beyond digital, companies can—and must—do things differently. They enable—and require—companies to rethink the unique value they can offer customers. Digital technology doesn't just allow for doing things better but for doing better things—even generating whole new business models as companies reimagine their futures.

This is why, if you expected this book to be about "how to go digital," you will be disappointed; this is not that book. This book is about how all companies must rethink their place in a fundamentally changed world and how they must transform to build advantage that is sustainable.

The path taken by Best Buy, and by all the companies researched and profiled in this book, is in stark contrast to what many companies seem to be doing. Instead of incrementing their way toward an uncertain future, these leading companies set out to shape their future by serving a more ambitious and relevant purpose and fundamentally rethinking the system of capabilities that allows them to deliver on that purpose.

What has shifted? With product lifetimes shortening, organizations are recognizing that they can't sustain a differentiated position by focusing narrowly on products and services. Just because you have the best offerings today doesn't mean you'll have the best tomorrow. Smart companies now focus on building differentiation in what they do and how they operate, not just what they sell. If you get your differentiated capabilities right, then the flow of products, services, solutions, and experiences will follow.

Think about Apple's design capability, which has allowed it to disrupt every industry it entered, including computers, music devices, phones, cameras, and watches. Think about Amazon's retail interface design capability, which, through its sophisticated search, comments, linking, and online payment features, has been the driving force in moving almost every consumer category online. Think about Frito-Lay's rapid flavor innovation, which lets it quickly produce new ones when it senses demand—for instance, a mac 'n cheese flavor for Cheetos.

Technology plays an important role in all of these capabilities—but these capabilities are much more than just technology. They are highly integrated and often complex combinations of knowledge, processes, technologies, data, skills, culture, and organization models that together allow companies to create value in ways that others cannot. The complexity and need for integration make capabilities hard to replicate, which is why companies that define themselves through what they do tend to be distinctive and create lasting advantage.[1]

The Speed Trap

When we set out to describe what was so different about the beyond digital age, one of our colleagues said, "If I hear someone talk about the increasing rate of change one more time, my eyeballs will roll so much the muscles will cramp. *Future Shock* was published in 1970.[a] That's the year the Beatles broke up."

People pay attention to change because it is new and ignore continuity because it is not new, just as few pay attention to the electric or water utility until there's a blackout or a leak. But as Amazon's Jeff Bezos said in a 2012 fireside chat, "I very frequently get the question: 'What's going to change in the next 10 years?' And that is a very interesting question; it's a very common one. I almost never get the question: 'What's not going to change in the next 10 years?' And I submit to you that that second question is actually the more important of the two—because you can build a business strategy around the things that are stable in time."[b]

The first thing that comes to people's minds when they describe this new age is *speed*, but that's a facile diagnosis for the more interesting and multifaceted phenomenon that we explore in this book. And "speed" is not just a simplistic diagnosis but a dangerous one, because it can lead to the wrong prescription: become the

In the beyond digital world, the future will belong to companies that are willing to shed past belief systems and define new, much bolder value propositions. It will belong to companies that work with others in networks and ecosystems that create value in ways that no single organization can achieve alone and that continuously push the boundaries of what's possible. It will belong to companies that have clear and honest answers to two fundamental questions:

fastest hamster in the wheel. If all you do is increase speed, you will just make the same mistakes faster.

You will need to look for the things that *don't* change quickly—the massive problems in the world that need to be solved, the fundamental wants and needs your customers have and will continue to have, the unique things your organization is able to achieve.

To be clear, speed is an important factor, just not the way people generally think. They focus on externally driven speed (how fast things are changing), when the real issue is how quickly you can make decisions internally. People focus, in particular, on incredibly rapid change in technology, when the far bigger issue is the pace of business model disruption, which while often driven by technology typically occurs far more slowly.

If you use the things that don't change quickly as an anchor for your organization, you can channel your efforts to the areas that matter most to your customers and the problems you're solving. Doing so will allow you to get in front of change and to shape your own future. Instead of forever reacting to external forces, you will take control and create the change you want to see.

a. Alvin Toffler, *Future Shock* (New York: Random House, 1970).
b. https://www.youtube.com/watch?v=O4MtQGRIIuA.

"What unique value do we contribute in today's world?" and "What capabilities allow us to create that value better than anyone else?"

The problem is that this is all easier said than done. Building truly differentiated capabilities does not happen overnight, and you cannot expect to create value in this new capabilities-driven way while operating in an old model. Transforming your company to create value in this new way in the midst of a disruptive era is a *big* task. It requires leaders who challenge every dimension of their company: its purpose, its business model, its operating model, and its people. And it requires leaders who are willing and able to challenge themselves and question the fundamental ways in which they have operated so far.

The good news is that it can be done. We've seen it done in our own consulting work and in that of our colleagues. We've also seen it in the success and evolution of the companies we studied in depth for this book. Competing in industries as diverse as finance and pharmaceuticals, jewelry and software, aviation and construction, these companies have pivoted their strategies based on building their differentiated capabilities and have shown the power of moving beyond digital.

Twelve Beyond Digital Companies

To get to the heart of how established companies successfully compete as they go beyond digital, we conducted a three-year study (2018–2021) of businesses that had undergone significant transformative changes and succeeded. We started with a broad survey of industry peers and experts to identify established companies in their industry sectors they most respected for their ability to set a new strategic direction and execute on it. From the dozens of companies suggested to us by these industry experts, we used several criteria to select as our subjects the twelve companies listed below. We looked at whether they had undertaken significant business transformations and the correlation between their transformation and sustained business success thereafter. We ensured that they came from a range of industries and regions. We made sure the companies we studied included some that emerged from difficult times, as well as some that transformed from a position of strength. Finally, we chose companies where the leadership teams were willing to open up and share their insights and experiences via in-depth interviews over a number of sessions.

We will tell the stories of the twelve companies we studied in detail in the chapters ahead, but here's a preview:

Philips, the Amsterdam-headquartered multinational originally founded as a light bulb manufacturer in the late nineteenth century, exited its leading businesses in lighting and consumer electronics and reoriented its future around combining its know-how in manufacturing medical devices with emerging technologies and health-care solutions capabilities. As a result, Philips is transforming health outcomes for billions of people across the planet.

Hitachi, the Japanese conglomerate that had a products-based portfolio ranging from power plants to appliances to semiconductors, had been facing rapidly changing global market conditions and competitive landscapes. It reconfigured itself to focus on supplying what it calls "social innovation businesses" to improve quality of life across the world and create an environmentally conscious society. That reconfiguration led Hitachi to focus on five markets: IT, energy, industry, smart life, and mobility, building on the company's strengths in information technology, operational technology, and products.

Titan, a leading watch manufacturer and part of India's Tata Group, reimagined India's jewelry industry through a powerful ecosystem play, allowing it to deliver artisanal quality and trust within a modern retail experience.

Eli Lilly, the US pharmaceuticals maker, was in danger when several of its biggest and most profitable drugs went off patent. It undertook a transformation to significantly improve its R&D success rate and time to market of healthy living therapies, which allowed it to return to a premier position in the industry.

Citigroup, the US global bank that had been a financial supermarket when the economic crisis of 2007–2008 nearly put it out of business, took a step back to redefine what the company was uniquely about and created Citi Holdings to hold and divest everything that did not fit its new identity. The company continues to build on that foundation and uses the disciplines it learned during the financial crisis to refresh its strategy and further transform its core business into a leading future-oriented digital global bank.

Adobe, a Silicon Valley pioneer known for its graphics software, supercharged its offerings and found new relevance by transforming its business model to a cloud-based subscription service. It then leveraged the resulting data and consumer insights to effectively create and run a digital business.

Komatsu, based in Japan, transformed from manufacturing and selling construction equipment into a leader in digitally enabled smart construction solutions, helping its customers dramatically improve productivity and safety.

Honeywell, the US-headquartered multinational conglomerate, saw how digitization could transform the highly competitive market for sales and service in commercial aviation. It created a Connected Aircraft business to change the way people communicate on and with planes to make flights safer, more productive, and more entertaining.

Microsoft, the software giant founded in Redmond, Washington, radically adapted to the cloud-first, mobile-first era. It went from being a technology provider licensing software and selling products to a business model based on customers' consumption of cloud services. The company now empowers organizations and individuals to improve their operations and experience of daily living. The change required Microsoft to undertake a huge organizational and cultural transformation to build and deliver at global scale a business where its success was driven by its customers' success.

Cleveland Clinic, a health care system known for innovation, has been expanding its leading patient care capabilities to more locations and more patients across the world and has spread learnings occurring anywhere in its growing ecosystem to improve the care it delivers everywhere.

Inditex, the Spanish multinational retailer, has long dominated the market for midpriced fashion apparel with its Zara brand, but recently transformed its operations to get ahead of competition to deepen and speed up its understanding of what customers want and better satisfy those wants by seamlessly integrating its physical stores and online sales channel.

STC Pay, Saudi Telecom's financial startup, created a highly successful fintech platform that provides innovative financial solutions, banking technologies, and digital experiences for Saudi businesses, citizens, and guest workers. STC Pay created unprecedented financial freedoms in a previously underserved Islamic banking system.

As different as their stories are, every one of these companies had to reimagine its industries and business models. Some reacted out of a position of strength; others faced an existential threat. But all of them saw that they had to compete in a new way in the beyond digital environment and decided to get out in front of change and shape their own future.

Our research into these twelve companies uncovered seven fundamental elements at the source of successfully transforming to compete in a beyond digital world that we believe can provide a powerful road map for how you can achieve enduring success. We describe them below, but first a little background about how the competitive dynamic has changed is in order (see "The Speed Trap").

A New Competitive Dynamic

The first task is to step back and rethink the very basics of what drives success today. This is not the long list of new technologies, trendy business models, and the latest tools and apps, but the fundamental ways in which competitive advantage has changed and become a new force for creating winners and losers.

The major changes we've witnessed can be segmented into three clusters: a revolution of demand, a revolution of supply, and a transformation in the larger context in which companies operate.

The Revolution of Demand

On the *demand side*, the internet has given customers visibility into a much wider range of choices, whether through individual companies' websites or through aggregators like Amazon, eBay, and Alibaba. That visibility has caused a massive increase in the number of competitors each company has, because customers can see and buy products and services from providers located anywhere around the globe. Online reviews have also dramatically increased customers' ability to comparison shop and to learn about the experience of other customers. There simply is no place to hide for companies that aren't both excellent and differentiated.

Customer loyalty and retention have declined as digital marketplaces make it easy for customers to reevaluate their choices with every new purchase and select the provider that offers the best value proposition.[2] While relationships are still valuable, they are increasingly hard to establish and maintain without real differentiation. The minimum thresholds for consumer expectations of trust, quality, experience, and value keep shifting as performance is constantly reassessed. Among other changes, customers are less and less likely to be willing to be the integrators. They want companies to pull everything together to solve a problem, not to have to piece the solution together themselves.

Customers across industries have responded to the larger set of options they can choose from with a constantly increasing set of evermore specific requirements. They use the plethora of communication channels not just to articulate their needs but to insist that those needs are met. Customers therefore don't align with simplistic segments anymore—and companies are dealing with a nearly infinite set of expectations.

Finally, customers have increased their demand for experiences that come with a product or service. The quality of the experience— from discovery to purchase to speed of delivery to any continuing service relationship—is often as important as the quality of the product or service itself.

This intensity of customers' preference and their increased visibility into value have raised the bar considerably for any enterprise— being "in the game" is not enough, and just trying to do what others do will increasingly lead to irrelevancy. The future is all about substantive differentiation and creating measurable and meaningful value.

The Revolution of Supply

On the *supply side*, although we still see remnants of the past, massive changes impact how companies compete.

First is the issue of scale. For decades, big companies could dominate by using the benefits of mass production, distribution, marketing, and back-office operations. Today, companies get easy access to that sort of scale without owning it. Consider how cloud computing has eaten into the back-office advantages big companies once had and how today's sophisticated manufacturing is much less capital-intensive than yesterday's. Small companies (often enabled by alternative financing methods) now compete head-on with established players. Just think about how fintech companies like Robinhood in the United States, N26 in Germany, or OakNorth Bank in the United Kingdom have impacted the financial services market. The power of incumbents has declined, and barriers to entry have been lowered.

Second, a decline in friction has significantly reduced what we might call barriers to cooperation. Thirty years ago, companies that wanted to exchange data electronically had to pay tens of thousands of dollars to set up dedicated lines of communication with select partners; now connecting with multiple partners—large and small—has become much easier. While friction is hardly eliminated, reducing costs and hassles has enabled the creation of ecosystems of companies and institutions that together offer value in ways that no player alone could ever aspire to do. This ecosystem-driven economy has many dramatic implications:

- The offering of significantly more ambitious value propositions that solve real customer problems (like addressing people's need for mobility or health care) and that put pressure on everyone else to do the same.

- The rise of platform providers like Alibaba and Amazon that have created significant network scale and pull to these ecosystems.

- The increasing specialization of companies that focus on what they are truly great at and partner with others to provide the rest. Just think about what it means to be good at marketing these days: analytics, web design, user experience design, digital asset management, paid search and social media engagement, public relations, branding, advertising, and much more. Easy access to specialized services raises the table stakes almost to the point where big, clumsy generalists cannot compete.

- More intense competition, because the ease of plugging into an ecosystem means everyone with a role in it has to be prepared to defend its place.

In addition, companies' ability to capture, store, and analyze data has allowed them to greatly improve the quality of all of their undertakings, whether with customers, with the supply chain, in manufacturing, and so on. Gaining scale in data, in fact, has become the driving force for many business initiatives, whether you're entering partnerships with companies that hold data you need or setting up customer interaction channels that give you better insights into what customers want or need.

The Transformation of Context

The third major change we've witnessed and that has changed competitive dynamics—the *context within which companies operate*—is that the world has become much more complex. While leaders in the past were often driven almost exclusively by profit motives, today's leaders need to balance a much larger set of factors when considering how they create value. They need to deliver value to customers, invest in employees, deal fairly and ethically with suppliers, ensure environmental sustainability, and support the communities in which they work, all while generating long-term value for shareholders.[3] No company today can afford not to have an ESG (environment, society, and governance) agenda that is integrated into the purpose the company will drive as it shapes its future. And stakeholders increasingly ask for transparency on companies' ESG impact, leading to the rapidly growing importance of nonfinancial reporting to assess the full value of a company or investment.

Companies must adapt to a world in which people increasingly want to work for organizations whose purpose connects to their personal values. They ask that their employers have a broader positive impact on the communities in which they operate. And they look to companies to help address some of the massive societal problems—for example, climate change, income inequality, unemployment, gender inequality, racism, or mental/emotional well-being—that threaten the world today.

The ever-increasing level of global connectedness, while creating significant opportunities, has also greatly raised uncertainty and exposure to risk. It is difficult to emerge unscathed from the impact of hurricanes, floods, wildfires, supply chain interruptions, trade wars, political turmoil, armed conflicts, pandemics, and many more, even if these events originate in regions far away from where you operate. Companies must face challenges that affect their customers' ability to spend, their employees' ability to perform, and their partners' ability to deliver.

Companies also face new and ever-changing regulations. Whether they aim to get climate change under control, to protect national economies, or take care of people's health during a pandemic, regulatory changes are inevitable and can have significant consequences.

. . .

These changes, of course, haven't happened overnight. One of the characters in Ernest Hemingway's novel *The Sun Also Rises* may have described the phenomenon most succinctly when he was asked how he had gone bankrupt: "Two ways," he said. "Gradually, then suddenly."[4]

How Leaders and Companies Must Respond

A revolution in demand, a revolution in supply, a transformation of the business context—all in less than half the span of a single career. How should companies respond? How should you respond as a leader? It's clear that the old playbook—bulk up to dominate, split up to "release value," run initiative after initiative to digitize or ratio-nalize your operations, or just get faster—is a response to the symp-toms, not to the underlying causes.

A deeper response is to react to the changed competitive dynamic and find fundamental new ways of creating value. What matters for success in today's world is building scale in a few capabilities that allow you to deliver value to your customers and the world at large in a unique and differentiated way, via new, digitally enabled eco-systems and platforms.

Zara, the flagship brand of Inditex, is an example of a company that reshaped its marketplace—midpriced fashion apparel—by competing in this capabilities-based way and by building on the full array of digital tools and technologies to evolve and scale their dif-ferentiating capabilities.

Apparel is one of the early markets in which the demand revolu-tion took hold. It's a hyper-competitive market with quickly changing consumer preferences and significant customer churn. Zara began to address this fashion trend head-on, decades ago. Rather than adopt-ing the traditional scale-based model of retail, the company pioneered a unique business model based on "fit to demand." Instead of com-mitting a large percentage of production for the next fashion season, Zara commits only a small amount and uses customer feedback and a highly responsive production network to replenish stores with new and different products twice a week. Zara goes against the conventional wisdom of mass production by producing small batches of garments and locating 60 percent of its manufacturing in proximity to its head-quarters in Spain in order to be more flexible. This allows the company to prototype new styles in just five days; and it can take a new garment as little as fifteen days to go from design and production to store shelves. The concept is phenomenally successful: Inditex began expanding globally in 1988 and today is the world's largest fashion retailer by revenue, selling in more than two hundred markets through its online platform and its over six thousand stores in ninety-six markets.

Zara's success is due to the powerful capabilities it has built and scaled across the company: deep customer insights; accurate fashion-forward designs; efficient response manufacturing and operations; and globally consistent and pervasive branding. These capabilities work together in a mutually reinforcing system, each dependent on the others and each making the others stronger.

Zara's leaders, however, don't rest on their laurels. They recognize that their revolutionary supply model needs to keep turning to keep pace with change. They have used digital to lift Zara's differentiating capabilities to a whole new level. Customer insights were tradition-ally gained by sales associates and managers directly observing and engaging with customers about what they liked, disliked, and would like to see in stock. That practice is still important but has been complemented by additional information. In 2014, Inditex's leaders deployed a new take on an old technology, embedding a cheaper, recyclable RFID chip in the security tag of every item Zara sells—something virtually unheard of at the time. This tag now allows indi-vidual tracking of garments from the logistics platforms until their ultimate sale, anywhere around the globe, instantly. That knowledge allows the organization to uncover fashion trends and create new waves of collections even more precisely than it could before. Jesús Echevarría, Zara's chief communication officer, recounts, "The RFID meant a huge step forward. It was the tool that helped our traditional 'fit-to-demand' model to be even more accurate. It helped stores locate the precise sizes in the right place and to update inventories in a very quick way. And definitely it was the solid basis for the fully integrated platform of stores and online policy marked by the CEO, Pablo Isla."[5]

Zara didn't stop there. The company also realized that RFIDs made distribution more efficient and in-store garment management more accurate, which in turn improved overall customer service stan-dards. It also enabled the full integration of all physical and online stores, something leadership did not even have in mind when they started looking into the broader application of the technology. But now, with e-commerce sales becoming more important, "in every country, the internet is the best store," says Iván Escudero, head of RFID and Integrated Stockroom:

> The internet is the macro store, where all the collections are. Customers have changed significantly: they see something they like on the internet, they go into a store, and they may be disappointed if the garment is not there. So, every store now is a picking point for internet orders, and you can order from any store and have it shipped home. But that's only possible because of how we use RFIDs. RFIDs tell us exactly where the stock is, and thereby allow us to have a centralized stockroom. If there's an order nearby, we can move it from one point in the stockroom to a store and deliver it from the store to a final client.

Inditex is also changing its store concept: opening larger, high-tech stores; extending and modernizing existing stores; and consolidating smaller stores that are less well-positioned to offer customers these new, integrated services. It increasingly uses technology to simplify the shopping experience. RFIDs make it easy to locate the desired product, customers can book fitting rooms through their mobile app or in-store devices and continue shopping until they receive a message that a fitting room is available for them, and self-checkouts and mobile checkouts reduce waiting time.

In 2017, Zara launched a new pop-up concept with a novel shopping experience, first in London, and then in other cities. The pop-up location offers a select collection of items that can be purchased through Zara.com directly from the store and offers customers the ability to collect online orders and return or exchange items. Zara personnel are equipped with tablets that allow customers to purchase at any point in the store and pay at the till. And smart mirrors show items in real size to coordinate and combine items with other garments and accessories.

Covid-19 has accelerated many of the trends that shaped Inditex's integrated stores and online platform strategy. In June 2020, the company announced it would speed up and broaden its digital transformation. Over the next two years, it would invest €1 billion in bolstering the online business and a further €1.7 billion in upgrading the integrated store platform, deploying advanced technology solutions. The company would consolidate more than a thousand smaller stores that were less well positioned to offer these new customer experiences. "The overriding goal is to speed up full implementation of our integrated store concept, driven by the notion of being able to offer customers uninterrupted service no matter where they may find themselves, on any device and at any time of the day," Executive Chairman Pablo Isla said.[6]

As Zara shows, differentiating capabilities aren't just things functional leaders invest in. These capabilities must be at the core of your purpose because they define who you are as a company. They must deliver the value proposition you are promising to your customers. And they must be where an ever-increasing amount of your investment goes and where your talent is deployed.

The Seven Imperatives for Beyond Digital Leadership

For most established companies, creating lasting value in a beyond digital world requires transformation. But the kind of transformation required is not just about technology innovation. Yes, companies had to make sure they could reach customers digitally and enable employees to "go to work," but this accelerated wave of digital initiatives is mostly about staying in the game. No matter how many digital initiatives you implement, you can't expect to win by being the same as your competitors, which are all doing similar things (even if at different speeds).

So what do you need to do to transform successfully, and how do you do it? To supplement our experiences and prior research on how companies succeed, we researched in depth the twelve companies previously discussed. Note that we didn't just select successful companies to study what they had in common—an approach that many researchers have failed with in the past. We focused on established and substantial companies that applied the one approach we know (backed up by significant analytical research and many decades of hands-on client experience) that generates consistent results across time: shaping your company's future by building on a set of differentiated capabilities that deliver your company's unique value proposition.[7] We selected companies that followed this approach, and studied what they did and how they operated, to learn how they successfully keep their companies relevant and value generating in a beyond digital era.

Our objective was to learn not just about what these companies did, but about how they did it: how they made choices about the future, how they came to the insights that informed their choices, how their leadership teams worked, how they got people on board, and how they overcame the inevitable stumbles in their journeys.

We found that despite the differences in industry, geography, and size, the transformation journeys these twelve companies undertook and the way their leadership teams navigated the changes had key elements in common. They each started their journey with looking externally and reinventing their value proposition and their relationship with customers and partners. Then they undertook significant internal transformations to align how they operate and how they lead with their imagined future. And finally, the leaders of these companies took on themselves—their own beliefs, strengths, and weaknesses—so that they could be fit to shape their companies' future.

We summarize key insights from their journeys as seven leadership imperatives that together provide a powerful playbook for how to structure and execute the transformations that are required.

TABLE 1-1

The seven leadership imperatives for transforming your organization and how they differ from what companies typically do

	What companies typically do	Lessons learned from leading companies
How companies face the external world	Implement digital initiatives and adapt to customer and competitor moves.	**Reimagine your company's place in the world:** Shape your own future by redefining what significant problems your company is here to solve and what differentiating capabilities you will need to build to deliver on that promise.
	Source elements of their value chain from suppliers, distributors, and other third parties.	**Embrace and create value via ecosystems:** Collaborate with other organizations—including, in some cases, competitors—to deliver value propositions that no company could offer by itself. Focus on what you do best and combine that with the capabilities, speed, and scale your ecosystems enable to generate greater value for all participants.
	Invest in data analytics to better understand customer behavior.	**Build a system of privileged insights with your customers:** Build trusted relationships with customers to get unique insights on their true wants and needs. Be willing to source and share data to accelerate your ability to create differentiating insights. Compete on the basis of those insights to get in front of change and continuously improve the value you create.
How companies set themselves up to build fundamental advantage	Organize in matrix models of functional and business-unit specialization and set up cross-functional projects to deliver change initiatives.	**Make your organization outcome-oriented:** Bring together multidimensional skills in outcome-oriented teams that deliver the differentiated capabilities that drive the future of the organization. Place those teams at the heart of your operating model and rewire your organization's DNA to enable the new ways of working.
	Give experienced leaders strong top-down authority to deliver results in their individual areas.	**Invert the focus of your leadership team:** Rethink the roles, skills, and power structures on the leadership team to drive collaborative performance. Install governance mechanisms that shift the team's focus to propelling the transformation together.
	Implement change and communications programs to overcome change resistance and incentivize people to take the journey.	**Reinvent the social contract with your people:** Center your transformation on your people, reassuring them of the intrinsic value of humans in a world of automation and giving them the freedom and means to take leadership in the transformation. Create a system of engagement focused on purpose, contribution, community, and rewards beyond pay.
How leaders rethink themselves	Build on their strong suits as leaders to drive important changes.	**Disrupt your own leadership approach:** Recognize the need for a new type of multifaceted leadership, where strengths need to be balanced across a range of leadership paradoxes.

We'll go into detail in the chapter on each that follows, but here is a bit about how the winning companies we've researched put each of the imperatives into practice.

Reimagine Your Company's Place in the World

To succeed in the beyond digital world, you need to take a stand on what position your company is going to occupy. You need to take a leap of imagination to look beyond your current portfolio of businesses and products and beyond what your competitors are doing to imagine who you want to be. You need to define your company's place in the world in terms of the unique value you create for customers and for society and the system of distinct capabilities that allows you to create that value in ways that others cannot. If your company vanished off the face of the Earth, how big a hole would you leave for your customers and society?

The value you're creating, in many cases, will be significantly more ambitious than what companies could have imagined just five to ten years ago. That's because it's much easier for them to collaborate toward a common goal and because the evolution of platforms and ecosystems has made it possible for them to choose more purposefully what they're going to focus on and in which areas they can access another organization's capabilities. This is not just true for the largest organizations. Any company—and every company—has the opportunity and, we believe, the requirement to take on a bolder and clearer vision for what part of customers' lives or businesses a company will help address.

Coming up with a powerful place combines art and science. Looking at trends and asking customers what they want is no longer enough. You need to get in front of change by developing a point of view on how value will be assessed and created in the future. You need to understand how regulatory, societal, environmental, and technology changes may impact the future. You need to recognize what you do uniquely well and how you can leverage those strengths to create unique value. You need to identify how different value propositions could help you shape demand and how those value propositions would do in the face of external shocks. You will then need to make a bold choice about which value proposition gives you a right to win and that will determine your place in the world.

Once you've defined your company's place in the world, you need to reimagine the capabilities needed to deliver on that place. To do this, rethink end-to-end what you need to do to fulfill your value proposition. Be clear about how technology decisions should support your capabilities, rather than playing the game of investing in everything. Focus your energy on how digital can help you improve the value you have promised to deliver.

Embrace and Create Value via Ecosystems

Trying to compete on your own will not only limit the value-creation opportunities available to you but also make it impossible for you to gain deep customer insights and to scale up quickly enough the critical capabilities that are required. For companies big and small and in whatever industry, going it alone will only increase the risk of being left behind.

Many of today's problems are so massive that no single company can solve them on its own. They can be tackled only by networks of companies and institutions that work together. And the era of asking customers to be the integrator is over. Customers expect—and demand—that suppliers work together to deliver integrated solutions.

Given the pace of change, companies need to quickly scale up capabilities. They don't have the time—or the financial resources— to build all of the required capabilities on their own. The only way for companies to thrive in this disruptive age is to work with ecosystems to access the capabilities that others have built—and do it at speed, at scale, and flexibly.

Making your ecosystem strategy work isn't easy. The level of complexity is admittedly higher. It's not enough to worry about your own value realization, you also have to be concerned about how your ecosystem partners are doing. And you can expose your company to real risks by opening up access for your ecosystem partners to your data, intellectual capital, and talent. But the risks and effort are worth it, because competition will increasingly be won or lost based on ecosystems.

Build a System of Privileged Insights with Your Customers

Understanding your customers, while always important, is taking on a whole new urgency. They want change more quickly, and their needs and desires have become more granular. At the same time, opportunities for data collection, storage, and analysis have exploded. If you don't take advantage, you'll fall behind.

Building a system of privileged insights with your customers requires much more than just buying market research. It requires companies to establish a foundation of purpose and trust, because customers share their most useful information only if the value you offer resonates with them and they trust you to make good use of the information. It requires companies to lay out a purposeful customer insights strategy and road map to focus their efforts on solving their customers' most important problems. It requires companies to "listen" to customers across the entire spectrum of their interactions by making mechanisms for gaining insights an integral part of how they operate. And it requires companies to wire their privileged insights into how they work by using them to systematically strengthen their value proposition, capabilities system, and the products and services they offer to remain sustainably differentiated.

Gaining privileged insights may become one of your most important capabilities given its importance to value creation and sustainable differentiation. The better your insights, the more you can improve your value propositions in a way that is relevant for customers; the more you improve your value propositions, the more trust you generate by delivering on your promises and the more customers engage with you; the more customers engage with you and trust you, the more you remain connected with and relevant to them—no matter what changes are happening in the world around you. And to those that fear the constant shift of customer behavior and how to stay relevant, developing this capability will be the best antidote for falling behind, or better, the best tool to continue to shape your value proposition going forward.

Make Your Organization Outcome-Oriented

Creating value by scaling up a few differentiating capabilities requires a new model of working and teaming given the likely gigantic lift some of these capabilities will require as you deliver a bolder value proposition. You can't get away with plucking people out of their functional roles and asking them to work together 10 or 20 percent of their time, or for six weeks or six months. The typical cross-functional teams are no match for the dedication, focus, and energy required to bring your value proposition to life. Instead, you will need to build more durable outcome-oriented teams that deliver your differentiating capabilities by bringing together what they need from across the organization.

Creating these teams starts with identifying the few things that are most important to get right to deliver on your value proposition. What expertise, knowledge, technology, data, processes, and behaviors must you bring together to be able to deliver that output? This sort of thinking will let you shift from the old functional and fixed organization to a model of outcome-oriented teams that work across organization boundaries to deliver your capabilities.

These teams will coexist with the corporate center, business units, and functions/shared services, but will increasingly become more prominent elements of the organization. Their leaders will have a seat on the top team equal to that of their corporate, functional, and business unit peers. Many functional experts will be embedded within the outcome-oriented teams and rotate across functions and business units to develop broader skills and collaborative ways of working. In the capabilities-based organization, purely functional teams become more focused on the delivery of monofunctional work as well as the development of functional methods and procedures and driving functional talent development across the organization. Business units in this new model become even more customer- and market-centric (and less product-centric), and as such will play an important integration role to ensure capabilities are appropriately shaped toward customer needs.

Changing the lines and boxes alone isn't going to get your organization to work in this new collaborative way. You will need to address your organization's DNA by changing how you allocate investment and how you do planning and budgeting; rethinking what's measured and rewarded; putting in place career models that make the fluid organization a reality; and facilitating the change by shaping new behaviors.

Invert the Focus of Your Leadership Team

Just as your company needs a strategic effort to build the right differentiating capabilities, your leadership team will need new skills and mechanisms to shift to this new form of value creation.

You will need to step back and start thinking from a clean sheet: Do we have the right roles? Do we have the right people? Are we focusing on the right things? Are we driving the transformational change required or spending most of our time responding to the organization's short-term needs? Are we working together effectively?

Our research identified three significant actions that help leadership teams drive the transformation agenda:

- Establish your top team based on the right skills mix, rather than tenure. What roles, skills, and backgrounds are needed to deliver the capabilities you have chosen to focus on and deliver on your reimagined place in the world?

- Shift your leadership team's focus toward driving the transformation, not just responding to today's demands. What structures and mechanisms will allow you to ensure the urgent does not overwhelm the important?

- Take ownership for how your leadership team collaborates and behaves. How do you best instill the level of shared accountability and collaboration your place in the world demands?

Reinvent the Social Contract with Your People

Engaging employees in executing a transformation has always been important, but it's now taking on a whole new meaning. Given the increasing reliance on capabilities that people help innovate and the rapid pace of change, there is no way the leadership team can shape the future on its own. The only way to succeed is to adopt a "citizen-led approach"—to have employees deep inside the organization and the ecosystem keep abreast of what's going on around them and continuously contribute and innovate in a way that is in line with where the company is headed.

You will need to fundamentally rethink the "contract" you have with those people, so they bring their best to work every day. We don't mean the legal document that states the terms of employment, but the implicit contract between the company and its people that makes sure that both parties get what they need to thrive.

To get people to own where the company is headed, you will need to reassure them of their importance in shaping the company's future, even in a technology-dominated world. Digitization and automation raise fear among workers that they're going to be replaced with robots.

Be clear that people are—and will continue to be—at the center of your capabilities system and will continue to be needed to harness technology in innovative ways.

Once people understand their role, engage them meaningfully: connect their purpose to the company's purpose; make sure they can contribute and be part of the solution; give them a sense of community; help them develop the skills and experiences they need (including the ability to use technology more effectively); and give them the time and resources required to build the company's differentiating capabilities.

Reinventing the social contract isn't an exercise meant to make employees feel good (though it will!). It's about getting employees and the ecosystem to choose to be on board to help you transform the company. You will need to be even clearer about where your organization is headed so your people can see how everything you do fits together and can contribute to determining how—together—you're going to get there.

Disrupt Your Own Leadership Approach

Navigating the shifting landscape of the world beyond digital presents different challenges than leaders faced just five or ten years ago—it requires a new form of leadership. The leaders we interviewed for our research consistently emphasized that they undertook a journey of personal transformation that was every bit as exciting and arduous as the one their companies took. The very nature of the transformation required bold thinking and action across the range of decisions we've articulated.

Despite the specificity of each company's—and each leader's—development journey, we have observed a common set of characteristics that leaders had to address. Today's successful leaders need to be both strategists and executors. They need to be tech-savvy and deeply human. They need to be good at forming coalitions and making compromises, all while being guided by their integrity. They need to be deeply humble and know their limitations and at the same time show the way and make big decisions. They need to constantly push for innovation while being grounded in who they are as a company. And they need to be globally minded as well as deeply rooted in their local communities.

We're not suggesting that leaders need to excel in all areas, but being strong in just a few and weak in others will expose challenges in leading a transformation of this magnitude. So while you will build on your strengths, being deeply aware of this set of characteristics will help you be deliberate about your development, seek the right experiences, and surround yourself with the right people who will round out your leadership profile.

How the Seven Imperatives Fit Together

The seven imperatives are so intertwined that it would be very difficult to pick just two or three to focus on. Consider what happens if you overlook one of them. When you aren't clear about your company's place in the world, for example, you won't have a clear purpose that's rooted in how you create value for customers. You'll lack a North Star for making decisions about who's in your ecosystem and how you should partner with those organizations. When you don't build a system of privileged insights with customers, you won't understand how their wants and needs evolve and you won't know how to evolve your place in the world to keep it fresh and relevant to the customers you care about most. When you don't make your organization outcome-oriented, your people will have issues working across organizational silos and will struggle to build and scale the differentiated cross-functional capabilities needed to fill your place in the world with life. If you overlook any of these imperatives, you won't be able to address the others successfully.

On a positive note, however, working on any one of those imperatives helps your efforts in the others. Working in an ecosystem, for example, allows you to glean deeper insights into more customers from more angles. You can also combine forces with ecosystem partners, offer greater value to customers, and occupy a more ambitious place in the world. And you strengthen the capabilities of your leadership team by giving them a chance to see intimately how other companies work. In a similar spirit, reinventing the social contract with your people and engaging them meaningfully enables them to contribute to shaping both where your company is headed and how it's going to get there. People at the front lines will have a way to feed back what they're learning about customers and make sure those insights inform how the company is evolving. They will find ways to improve how they work together in teams, further breaking down the traditional organizational silos.

We can't stress enough the importance of being clear about the differentiating capabilities your company will need to build. Capabilities are the bridge between your reimagining your company's place in the world and your ability to fill that place with life. Being very clear about your differentiating capabilities is a prerequisite for working with your ecosystem because you will have a powerful framework for determining what you do versus what others provide. Gaining privileged insights in most cases will become one of your differentiating capabilities, keeping your value proposition fresh and relevant. Your differentiating capabilities will determine what outcomes will be most important for your organization to deliver and what leaders you will need on your top team to enable the organization to do so. And being clear about your differentiating capabilities will also steer your people's efforts and innovation toward the areas where they are most needed. You, too, will see how to shape your own transformation as a leader so you can lift those capabilities to world-class level.

Our experience is that most companies will have significant work to do in most of these areas. Tackling one or two won't be enough, but often organizations seek to simplify the work ahead and don't confront the underlying gaps that likely exist in all areas. Working on all seven imperatives creates a true interlocking system that's going to make your company fit for the challenges ahead.

A Road Map

We do not hold up the seven imperatives as the only path to success. But they do form a powerful and comprehensive path that helps leaders truly ensure the relevance of their company's place in the world, fill that place with life, and build the transformational muscle that will allow them to stay relevant over time. It is also an appealing path that feels intrinsically rewarding. Rather than constantly trying to react to what your growing set of competitors does, you can gain control, get in front of change, and shape your own future.

Each of the next seven chapters describes one of the imperatives that leaders need to address. Chapters 2 through 4 deal with your company's interaction with the external world; 5 through 7 turn to your internal interactions; chapter 8 is about your personal journey as a leader; and chapter 9 shares some important lessons learned about how to shape your company's journey.

This journey isn't going to be easy, and it isn't going to happen overnight. But it is a deeply rewarding one. And it is going to be at the heart of your legacy as a leader.

Let's start now.

2

Reimagine Your Company's Place in the World

There is no passion to be found playing small and settling for a life that's less than the one you're capable of living.

—Nelson Mandela

Ten years ago, the Amsterdam-headquartered multinational Philips was a conglomerate with a sprawling portfolio of businesses that ranged from audio and video consumer electronics to lighting and medical equipment. Philips had a distinguished history. Founded as a light bulb manufacturer in 1891, it pioneered electric shavers in the mid-twentieth century, invented the audio cassettes that were ubiquitous from the 1970s into the 1990s, and codeveloped (with Sony) the compact disc in 1982. The company also made medical devices, starting with pioneering X-ray technology during World War I and innovating in imaging technologies such as computed tomography (CT) and magnetic resonance imaging (MRI) machines for hospitals.

By 2011, Philips Electronics, as the company was then known, had become the largest lighting company in the world, a leading player in consumer electronics, and one of the top medical device manufacturers—an electronics giant diversified across industry sectors. Yet it was hemorrhaging jobs and money, laying off thousands of workers, and posting a €1.5 billion loss.

Under new CEO Frans van Houten, Philips looked into the future and decided to reimagine itself fundamentally. The company would refocus itself around health care and healthy living and pursue a truly ambitious goal: "to make the world healthier and more sustainable, with the goal of improving the lives of 2.5 billion people a year by 2030."[1]

Philips would transform into a health technology company enabling integrated health-care solutions and services that unlock the power of data and AI at the point of care and optimize delivery across the health continuum—from healthy living and prevention of illness through diagnosis, treatment, and aftercare. The transformation would bring together Philips's deep consumer insights and capabilities, its depth in medical device technologies, and the power of data and AI to transform the cost and quality of health care and healthy living.

Today, the company's technology-enabled offerings include wearable personal devices to help manage a healthy lifestyle; precision diagnostic solutions augmented with AI to accurately diagnose health issues and support the right treatment; minimally invasive treatment solutions to help address a medical condition accurately and safely; and home care monitoring and services to support a fast return to healthy living.

Philips built its new place in the world on two pillars: (1) an unmet need for people to manage their health care and well-being in a more integrated way and (2) strong capabilities in medical devices, consumer insights, and technology innovation. Van Houten explains:

> In health, we were competing on technology products that
> were advanced, and we had a leading position. But we also

saw the digital data revolution coming, and that value would have to come more out of understanding the data rather than only creating the data. It would therefore require a massive transformation to really impact the world of health. And that was the point where I recognized that the chances that we would transform lighting and health care simultaneously were not so high. And so we made a choice. We created a vision of where health care is going. We said we will leverage Philips's insights in consumers, with the insights that we have in health care and in clinical technology. And we will improve the lives of billions of people across the planet.

Philips's new place in the world drew on research showing the promise of value-based health care to improve outcomes and lower overall costs. (Value-based care compensates health-care providers for achieving successful patient health outcomes, as opposed to the traditional "fee-for-service" approach that compensates based on the volume of procedures performed.) Philips jumped on that insight and established the "health continuum" as its guiding framework. This framework characterizes a person's movement from healthy living and prevention of illness to accurate and timely diagnosis, appropriate treatment, care and monitoring in the home, and hopefully, back into healthy living. Philips's goal was to play across this continuum and make the promise of health care and healthy living real. Van Houten recalls,

> When we plotted our existing activities on the health continuum, we started to look for, "How do we connect everything?" If you only compete on the basis of products, that has its limitations. It's much more powerful to be able to provide solutions which revolve around the question, "How do we keep people healthy?" or "If you fall sick, how do we diagnose you first time right?" or "If you get diagnosed, how do we treat you in a way that is minimally invasive and gets you to

recover faster?" And then, "How do we support people with a chronic disease so that they can live a decent life in their own community and their home?"

This was a very different approach for Philips. As former Chief Innovation and Strategy Officer Jeroen Tas describes it,

> In the old days, we focused on products. We used to have the best in cardiovascular ultrasound. We also did cardiovascular detection of disease on the CT. We had sixteen-lead ECGs [a cutting-edge technology for electrocardiograms]. You can go on and on. All of those had been developed in isolation and for a pretty narrow purpose. But now, if it's about outcomes, we have to look at our business completely differently than we did in the past. You may still have a great CT machine, but the race is not going to be the next great technical feature. The race is going to be, "How can I create a better diagnosis?" "How can I make a better patient experience?" "How can I give the radiologists and clinicians a way better experience?" But most importantly, "How can I contribute to a way better outcome for the patient?"

Looking at health care from a patient's journey point of view rather than from a product point of view led Philips to appreciate the need to develop platforms and to leverage data, informatics, and workflow automation. Van Houten explains: "We believe that the silo of radiology and the silos of pathology, molecular biology, and genomics all need to come together in an integrated way so that you can have one view of what's wrong with the patient, completely in agreement. Then you can use AI and digital technologies to select the right treatment pathway. That's the holy grail." In van Houten's view, this platform approach can create real value for patients and higher productivity in the delivery of care.

Today, by addressing health care as a "connected whole," Philips can unlock gains and efficiencies and drive innovations that help deliver on its quadruple aim: enhancing the patient experience, improving health outcomes, lowering the cost of care, and improving the work life of care providers.

Philips's new mission guided the company through a series of transformations that revolutionized its portfolio, business model, and culture. These changes meant radical restructuring, including an exit from legacy businesses that had long been a part of the company's identity. Starting in 2011, Philips sold off its TV, audio, and video operations; spun off its lighting division into a new company, Signify N.V.; and completed its major divestments in 2021 when it sold off its domestic appliances business. (Some of those businesses continue to produce and market Philips-branded products.) Philips reorganized around customer domains, bringing together previously siloed functional teams to create customer outcomes, build ecosystem partnerships, and bring in new talent to take its technology, data, and software capabilities to new levels. Today, Philips's focus as a health technology player has resulted in remarkable gains in profitability and shareholder value, with the stock price rising 82 percent in the five years ending in 2020.

Philips, which has positioned itself to compete in what promises to be one of the most vibrant industries of the twenty-first century, is a great example of the reimagination that organizations have to do to shape their own future.

Why Reimagining Your Company's Place Is Critical

Reimagining your place in the world has become a prerequisite to securing your relevance in the future. Reimagination defines the compelling value you will offer and how you create that value in a differentiated way. Both dimensions—the unique value you promise *and* the differentiating capabilities that allow you to deliver that promise better than anyone else—are what defines your company's place. Focusing on just one of those dimensions isn't enough. Philips couldn't just declare that it wanted to improve the lives of people through better health care. It needed to define the unique capabilities that would enable it to deliver on that goal, building on a differentiated set of capabilities it already had (e.g., deep clinical and technical understanding of medical imaging technologies) and focusing on building new differentiated capabilities (e.g., predictive diagnostics enabled by AI). Combined, these two dimensions provide a powerful frame for *what* the organization does to create value and *how* it does it—which is critical in the beyond digital world, where trust and outcomes are not only sought after but increasingly demanded.

As we discussed in chapter 1, the revolution of demand, the revolution of supply, and the changing context within which businesses operate are shifting customer expectations for value and how that value is created. With a very different model of how to be successful and the need for businesses to help solve society's biggest challenges, most existing companies will have to redefine their place in the world.

But even for companies that have not (yet) felt the full weight of these changes, it would be unwise to just digitize what they're currently doing or increment their way to the future. Yes, you'll keep becoming more efficient, but so will your competitors, and the gains will be competed away. You may stay "in the game" in a market that hangs on to some relevance, but most probably you'll increasingly struggle to maintain your position as others gain in prominence. Some companies may think that their age-old value propositions, strong brand, longtime reputation, and loyal customers will remain relevant. But customers increasingly look for the unique value you're providing now versus what you were known for in the past, and over time others may see your lack of lasting advantage as an opportunity to innovate. And as ESG considerations reshape how value is perceived and measured, all companies must reexamine how the value they offer remains contemporary and relevant. Therefore, even if you don't see an immediate threat as the nature of competition and the external environment changes, that state isn't going to last, so use the relative stability you have now to rethink how you shape your future.

So, what does real differentiation look like in today's environment? Nearly all examples of true advantage in today's market derive from powerful differentiated capabilities, the few things a company does better than anyone else. These capabilities—like Zara's ability to produce on-trend merchandise quicker and more precisely than most retailers—are inherently complex. That's because any great capability typically combines knowledge, processes, technologies, data, skills, culture and organization models, and integrating work across functions to create the right outcomes is particularly challenging (as we'll discuss in chapter 5). While complexity is often considered a detriment, this type of complexity offers particular value in today's environment, as it enables you to advance your place in the world and can be a tremendous barrier for competitors to emulate your success.

But there's much more than complexity—capabilities in fact represent a new form of scale and carry a strong microeconomic advantage. Whereas the sheer size of their business once gave companies an advantage, what matters today is the scale of their differentiating capabilities. Capabilities today typically require significant (often fixed) investment, particularly in data, technology, and people. Just consider the investment it takes to make your supply chain "intelligent" or to build a pricing capability that requires significant data, analytics, tools, and talent.

While these investments can seem daunting at first, when focused and when central to what you do, they can give you massive competitive advantage, not only because they enable you to do something that matters to customers better than anyone else but because they have the potential to propel your company forward in a self-reinforcing, virtuous loop: the better your differentiating capabilities, the more you win in the market as customers see the unique and relevant value proposition brought to life; and the more you win in the market, the more scale is brought to each capability. That virtuous loop can be made stronger as you expand your products and services to other

37

parts of your reimagined place in the world (and even to smaller businesses that otherwise would never have the scale required to access these capabilities) or as you "rent" those capabilities to your ecosystem partners. Building this kind of *relevant* scale will protect you from competitors who'd like to enter your space without having the required capabilities. Consider Frito-Lay's Direct Store Delivery (DSD) capability that enables it to deliver with high frequency and gain influence over the store shelf. This capability is particularly beneficial when launching new products or brands as it allows the company to gain rapid feedback from the market on what works well and what doesn't. That is information that others would have to pay a lot of money for. And while Frito-Lay developed this capability mainly for its snacks business, it can also use it to benefit smaller categories like dips—businesses that could likely not afford it on their own.

Building this capabilities engine requires you to be very clear about the few strengths that deserve your full attention and investment focus. You need to stop focusing on the size of your business or other independent assets and start defining yourself by what you do and the power of this new form of capabilities scale. But unless you clearly define your place in the world, your organization won't amass the scale behind the capabilities that both matter and provide competitive differentiation, and you'll end up being average at many things but great at nothing. With your place sharply defined, however, you can use your value proposition to keep you focused on the right system of capabilities—and to clearly stake out your place.

Let's look at one more example of a company reimagining its place before diving into how you can do the same.

Hitachi: Reimagining Its Place around Social Innovation Businesses

In 2009, Japanese multinational conglomerate Hitachi posted the biggest-ever annual loss by a Japanese manufacturer—¥787 billion, the equivalent of $8 billion—in the wake of the 2007–2009 global business downturn. At the time, Hitachi, which had been founded in 1910, had built up a vast and sprawling portfolio of businesses ranging in size from power plants to semiconductors and including well-known products like flat-screen TVs and computer storage devices.

According to Mamoru Morita, senior vice president and chief strategy officer,

> We were very strongly aware that there would be no future for us if we kept on doing business as usual. Our customers started to shift from making capital investments and buying products to a pay-per-use model. That meant that our existing business model of making high-quality products and having customers buy them would no longer work. That was also true in our infrastructure business, where we were sure we could gain more customers if we offered them contracts where they only pay for what they use. Railway operations in some places were like that. Customers wanted the rolling stock they would use that day brought to them in the morning, and they wanted to return it at night after they had finished using it. So we developed a subscription model for rolling stock in which Hitachi provides leasing, maintenance, and services in line with service-level agreements.

Takashi Kawamura, who had been chairman of Hitachi Maxell, took the helm as Hitachi's chairman, president, and CEO and put together an "emergency cabinet" to reshape the company. He brought Hiroaki Nakanishi—who had led a successful turnaround of Hitachi Global Storage Technologies in the United States and earlier had served as managing director of Hitachi Europe—on board. Nakanishi played a central role in the transformation, succeeding Kawamura as president in 2010 and then as CEO in 2014. "I think it was a big fortune for Hitachi that it was headed by Nakanishi, because he is someone who really believed in changing the company from the ground up," Morita says. "He was also clearly the type who urged everyone to get into action right away once something had been decided and think on their feet as things were moving along."

In July 2009, Hitachi announced its new growth strategy. "When we drew up our strategy, we deliberately started by laying out a broad direction and aligning the entire company around that direction, rather than getting slowed down in the details," comments Morita. "In times like today, when markets move so quickly, I think we would never be able to catch up with market changes if we had drawn up a detailed strategy."

The team began transforming Hitachi from a product-push company across many industries—including consumer businesses—into a global leader in social innovation, working with its customers and supplying advanced social infrastructure linked by IT that helps create social, environmental, and economic value. It would focus on industries with big social and environmental impact—for example, energy, mobility, or water treatment—and create value by adding its technology and innovation expertise to deliver solutions that "answer society's challenges." This has led Hitachi to evolve from manufacturing power plants and storage devices to helping car manufacturers improve their production chains and train operators reduce breakdown of their equipment.

Hitachi chose five markets to focus on: mobility, smart life, industry, energy, and IT. In each of these markets, Hitachi set out to understand in depth the issues that customers face and to develop solutions. For railway customers, for example, solutions included traffic control systems that help make train operations more efficient and improve passenger service by leveraging positioning information, operating information, and signal control; or breakdown prevention systems that use sensors on rail cars, doors, and compressors and enable parts to be replaced before a breakdown occurs. Hitachi also focused on digitizing the power grid (in energy), automating and electrifying production (in industry), over-the-air software update systems for vehicles (in smart life), and data-driven value creation in government (in IT).

"When formulating our growth strategy, we focused on adopting the customer's viewpoint and leveraging Hitachi's strengths," Nakanishi explained in a 2016 interview with the Japanese edition of *Harvard Business Review*. "We thought we should orient our business plan in the direction our customers were moving in. We then thought of how Hitachi could best contribute to its customers, and . . . we decided that we could combine IT [information technology] and OT [operational technology] and focus on social innovation businesses, supplying sophisticated social infrastructure systems. By providing solutions that combine IT and OT to create value, we can get closely involved in our customers' operations, and in this way, we can supply a wide range of additional related products."[2]

In order to focus the company on its new place in the world, Hitachi spun off its semiconductor business, withdrew from television manufacturing, and spun off its thermal power generation business. It also divested its hard disk drive (HDD) division—a move that shocked people, because Nakanishi himself had turned around the HDD business when he had been the CEO of Hitachi Global Storage Technologies in the United States. Given the new corporate strategy, though, Nakanishi concluded that the HDD business had little connection with Hitachi's newly defined place in the world. This decision sent an important message to the organization: *There will be no sacred cows.* Together with an ambitious cost-cutting program, these divestitures helped the company secure cash flow for investing in growth businesses.

The launch of the digital platform Lumada in 2016 was an important milestone. It was developed to connect the cyber and physical world and to provide actionable insights that help improve customers' performance and efficiency and thereby enable Hitachi to create more value for customers. "We felt it was the right thing for us to do because we had both the necessary IT and OT capabilities as well as the capability to handle the digital aspect of the platform properly in-house. And we had reached a certain size," comments Morita. "We're not interested in just sucking up data from customers all over the world and analyzing that data without a clear value proposition in mind. Our approach is to start by asking a company 'What value do you need to achieve?' and 'Why don't you join us to deliver that value?' Lumada allows us to collect the necessary data through sensors and other OT, analyze that data, and run digital simulations. And that enables us to create value by operating real things based on those results."

Solving a customer problem sometimes can't be done by Hitachi alone. The company will then partner with various third parties and give them access to Lumada—which not only solves an immediate problem but grows the ecosystem.

Toshiaki Higashihara, who succeeded Nakanishi as CEO in 2016, has continued the transformation of Hitachi and kept up the momentum. Under his leadership, the company acquired ABB's power grid business as well as GlobalLogic Inc. (a U.S.-headquartered digital engineering services company)—acquisitions worth more than $10 billion each—to offer greater value to more customers globally and to accelerate the company's digital solution business.

The company went from posting its record loss back in 2009 to record profitability in just two years. It transformed from an all-around conglomerate to a company focused on market-driven social innovation businesses. It transformed from a product company into a solutions provider, betting on its strengths in IT, OT, and products, including the development of its own Lumada platform, which now is the company's new core business. It achieved this by fundamentally reimagining its place in the world and ruthlessly executing a transformation that would enable it to fill that place.

How to Reimagine Your Place

As a reader of this book, you'll be very aware of the plethora of approaches, theories, and frameworks used to develop a business strategy. While many of those approaches may be individually useful, we believe strongly it is time to step back and address the most fundamental strategy questions of your organization, and to not compromise on the answers. The future requires extreme clarity both in the boldness of the challenges you seek to solve and in the specificity for how you will deliver the promises you make. By no means does this imply a lack of flexibility required in your strategy—but flexibility on its own is not a strategy we believe works in today's environment.

We'd strongly encourage you to begin by considering four insights from the companies we researched for this book.

Take a Point of View about the Future

Your job as a leader is not to maintain the status quo or to protect current profitability; your job is to create an organization that will succeed for decades. Doing so starts with developing a point of view about how the definition of value is changing. Companies today are being increasingly assessed against not just the amount of profit they generate for their shareholders, but also how they generate that profit (e.g., meeting net-zero carbon emissions commitments) and the broader value they generate for their employees (e.g., by offering equity in opportunity and compensation) and the societies in which they operate (e.g., by the impact on climate and solving meaningful societal challenges). And reporting requirements are also rapidly changing as regulators and investors across the world seek to enforce focus on these new broader measures of value, putting pressure on companies to reassess how they create value.

Being clear about this new definition of value is critically important, as it will not only be at the heart of how you shape your firm but also inform many other aspects of your organization's identity; for example, how you tell your value creation story to your customers and investors, how you report on your company's achievements, and how you engage your employees and ecosystem partners.

While the value you create for employees and society at large is key, the most important starting point for your place in the world is to define the fundamental customer needs you will address. This may sound simple, but few organizations today have this type of clarity.

Philips found that clarity and defined its place in the world when it set out "to make the world healthier and more sustainable, with the goal of improving the lives of 2.5 billion people a year by 2030." This sort of conviction, and the articulation of the difference your company is going to make in the world, will be key for motivating your entire ecosystem—your employees who will come to work to do amazing things, your partners who will support your value proposition, the financial markets that will provide you capital, and most importantly your customers, who will not only see great value in what you are doing for them but who will partake in the continuing improvement of what you offer. Could your conviction be wrong? Perhaps, but most companies have incredible insights about what customers need, and great leaders have the skills to home in on a real challenge that only their company can address. (See "Overcoming the Disincentives for Making Bold Decisions.")

Yes, the world is uncertain and will continue to remain uncertain, so you will have to build in flexibility. But all the leaders we interviewed ultimately had to stake out a clear position on how they believed value would be created in the future despite the uncertainty of the environment they faced. With Citigroup (whose story we share later in this chapter) and Inditex (see chapter 1), this theory of the future was based on strong views on what would *not* change (people will continue to need financial intermediation services and affordable yet quality fashion). In others, like at Philips and Hitachi, the clear position was based on a view of how value pools would shift

Overcoming the Disincentives for Making Bold Decisions

Ask an executive if they would like to build competitive advantage and you'll most certainly hear strong commitment to that task. Ask them to make bold decisions—to jettison businesses or build whole new capabilities—and you'll often encounter hesitation and doubt. Why do so few companies make these types of big choices? What holds them back?

In our research, we identified five reasons why these choices are so difficult for most CEOs:

- **Shareholder versus management incentives.** While share-holders can manage the risk around making big choices by holding a portfolio of investments, executives may have disincentives to pursue bold strategic alternatives. Executives aren't just concerned about whether making bold choices pays off on average, but whether a bold choice is going to pay off for their individual company or their own career.

- **Long-term versus short-term perspective.** Many executives perceive the time it takes big strategic shifts to pay off as exceeding the time horizon in which they need to demon-strate financial success. Market pressure for short-term results often delays or de-prioritizes major bets. Similarly, executives often perceive the future to be so uncertain that long-term investments may be misguided.

- **Perceived or real constraints.** CEOs typically inherit deci-sions, most notably relating to the portfolio of businesses (including geographic footprints). This inheritance can make

(continued)

clear strategic bets challenging, particularly when changes seem difficult for political or other reasons.

- **Inability to see a path from here to there.** Executive teams may recognize the need to transform their company and may know what to transform into but can't see a path to get from where they are today to where they want to be—for example, exiting a large, slow-growing business to free up investment for a business that's far smaller but has a much more promising future.

- **Once burned, twice shy.** In some cases, executives hold back because great strategic decisions in the past haven't been executed well, and they worry about taking on new, big moves. (We'd argue that the reason for strategies not being executed well is that often those strategies are not executable.)

Despite these challenges, we know many executives (including the ones we've interviewed for this book) who have indeed taken leaps of faith and have been rewarded for doing so.

If securing your rightful place in the world is not enough of a reason to make such a big bet, remember that there is risk in doing too little—a risk that executives don't always measure well. If you won't make big strategic decisions, there's a good chance that competitors will enter your markets by being willing to make bets you wouldn't.

The taxi industry is a good example. After global positioning and smartphone app technologies had undermined taxis' previous advantages around knowing how to navigate the streets and having a dispatching and hailing system, many taxi companies weren't left with much to wow their customers. Drivers and phone dispatchers weren't known for their courtesy. Vehicles weren't particularly clean. Companies didn't consistently deploy the latest technology. And cabbies and fleet owners saw little need to change because they felt that regulation would protect them against the threat of new entrants. This lack of real advantage had made the taxi industry highly vulnerable to disruption for years—but only recently, faced with ride-sharing companies, are many municipal cab companies raising their game by introducing hailing apps and improving other amenities.

How much better would it be for municipal cab companies if they had reimagined their place in the world and had begun transforming years ago?

The companies and executives that make bold decisions recognize that, despite all the uncertainty and volatility in today's environment, you can make choices that you won't regret no matter how the future unfolds. If you choose a strategic identity that is rooted in how you create unique value for customers, many of the choices you make are going to wind up being right no matter how the world shifts.

The discussion of risk is usually focused on, "What if we're wrong?" That's a reasonable question—but unwinding decisions is invariably easier and more productive than having never made the decisions in the first place. In fact, some portion of your investment should be spent on exploring and testing how fast the organization can move to its new place in the world and how far that place can extend. If you feel that the uncertainty is so great that you can't make a decision, you may be able to delay making a choice, possibly by partnering with another organization to rent capacity or capabilities you lack. But you can't let delay be a catch-all for avoiding decisions. If you delay everywhere, your lack of decision making will leave you without fundamental advantage, potentially weak

(continued)

in critical areas, and over time less and less relevant. And even though business model disruption may be slower than many people think—you could become prey for risk-oriented competitors.

from single-point products and services toward more integrated solutions that could deliver greater customer impact. In all cases, these points of view about the future were mostly the result of deep insight and experience with their respective markets. In some cases, where perceived external change was high, the companies evaluated multiple future scenarios to understand how they could help migrate their companies and their markets to the best outcome, and often found their reimagined place would thrive under multiple scenarios. Remember: it's not just about understanding the uncertainty that's hitting you; it's much more importantly about you helping shape that uncertainty.

Use Your Ecosystem to Widen Your Aperture

Your company is likely a participant in, or enabler of, several ecosystems. As illustrated by the Hitachi and Komatsu stories (described in detail in chapter 3), these ecosystems can be a rich source of insight into the real customer problems that need to be solved and the needs of the ultimate end user that must be addressed. Deeply understanding the ecosystems you participate in, how you contribute to them, and the integrated value they create can be a powerful source of insight to shape your thinking on your future place in the world.

Find Your Hidden Powers

There is likely something incredible your company is able to do that offers value far beyond your current products and services. Identify those capabilities that are unique and valuable and ask what else they could do to solve some of the big issues you see in your ecosystem. Amazon Web Services was initially a cloud capability intrinsic to Amazon's own business, until the company recognized how powerful it could be as a service for others. Organizations need to be brutally honest about what they bring to the table and question whether old beliefs of "We are great at . . ." still hold in today's environment. Great capabilities often outlast markets, products, and services, but they require upkeep, investment, and continuous innovation. The best place to start looking for your hidden powers is in businesses you own that are doing remarkably well. Behind every success, we invariably find a highly differentiated engine of advantage—a capability or a system of capabilities that work to drive those results. Ask the teams that are performing so well what's at the heart of that success and assess how that advantage may provide leverage in new ways.

Unconstrain Your Team

Reimagining your place is incredibly difficult when you let yourself be constrained by two factors: the decisions that your business has made in the past and the barrage of disruptive forces your team sees as unavoidably affecting the future of your organization.

Because of all the energy spent on keeping your current portfolio relevant, past decisions limit the options your leadership team is likely to consider. But what if your portfolio reflects an earlier value creation model (for example, bulk up to dominate) and isn't going to serve you well in the beyond digital world? As your leaders step back to reimagine your company's place in the world, they need to consider alternative futures, independent (at first) of how all of your businesses may or may not fit in that future. Yes, you'll have to create a road map for how to move from here to there and consider the impact of portfolio decisions, but don't start with those constraints.

Equally important is to separate true externalities from what your team can actually control. We often see leadership teams underestimating the time it is going to take a disruptive move to affect them and overestimating the effort and time it is going to take them to counter that move, resulting in a sense of fatalism. This distorted perception often results in leaders seeing change as something happening to them, rather than as something they can and should drive. To get out of that trap, make sure you start the reimagination of your place in the world not with what you think competitors are going to do but with what you are going to do to address fundamental problems or needs. For true externalities, like government regulation or macroeconomic conditions, take your team down the road of what they would do under a few scenarios. Understand how your reimagined place may or may not thrive under different realities, as well as the optionality you may need to build to deal with those outcomes.

With those lessons learned in mind, here are three steps for determining your future place in the world and staking out a strong (and adaptable) position.

Step 1: Envision Ideas for Potential Ways to Create Value

The starting point for reimagining your place is to define how value will be perceived and defined in the future. Generating value increasingly means more than realizing short-term profits and shareholder returns—it means generating value for customers, employees, and the societies in which you operate.

With that broader definition in mind, you can now start to identify ideas for how value could be generated. We recommend you do this via looking through three lenses.

Come up with a point of view on the future of your industry (or industries). Use your deep customer insights and your market expertise to come up with a point of view on the future and determine how you believe customer and end user needs are going to evolve, how megatrends (including ESG and technology trends) will impact value creation, and how value pools are going to shift. Here are some questions to think through:

- **What are the big problems in the industries and markets we serve that remain unsolved?** What are customers and end users really looking for? Are there pain points in the customer journey that need to be addressed (e.g., interfaces that are broken, information that doesn't flow, solutions that could be tailored to individual preferences)?

- **How is demand going to evolve?** How do megatrends like demographic changes, resource scarcity, or urbanization affect important customer and end user groups and their needs? What are the major industry-specific trends, and how do they impact what customers and end users want and need?

- **How will ESG requirements impact the future?** How is the perception of value going to change? What positive impact could we have on E, S, and G? What regulatory changes do we expect?

- **How is technology going to change what's possible?** How could technology revolutionize what we do and how we do things? Could there be a disruptor of our industry? If we had to break into our industry afresh, where would we start?

- **How are value pools shifting?** What does the end-to-end value chain/value network look like in the industry, and what steps are required to deliver value to the end user? What share of profit goes to each of those value chain steps/value network nodes? How is that going to change? Is there a technology-enabled disruption that could transform the value chain in unexpected ways?

Translate this point of view on the future into value generation ideas: What big problem could you solve? What fundamental customer needs could you address? How could you shake up the industry? What new value pools could you tap into?

For a food producer, for example, this first lens could lead to value-generation ideas like offering more plant-based (vs. meat-based) products to help reduce the carbon impact while offering more convenient and healthy food options in line with consumers' desires.

Look at archetypes and potential analogs from other companies and industries. Consider the common strategic archetypes for creating value—we call these *puretones*. Strategy& developed them in a research effort begun in 2008 and later published these ideas in the book *The Essential Advantage*.[3] These puretones reflect the basic value creation strategies of companies around the world and can help you understand if a particular value proposition may be relevant for your business. Some of these have become more prevalent in the recent past—for example, *platform providers* such as Amazon and Facebook, or *disintermediators* such as Uber or Waze. Others have lost relevance—for example, *category leaders* or *consolidators*. Still others have remained strong throughout—for example, *value players* such as IKEA or Walmart. (For a complete list, see the appendix, where we describe seventeen different puretone ways to play, companies that exhibit those ways to play, and how the new competitive dynamic has impacted each of these plays.) You can use these puretones as reference points as you set out to identify possible ideas for how you might create value in your industry. You may also be able to learn from analogs, looking at other industries that have experienced similar dynamics as yours.

For our food producer above, this second lens could lead it to consider becoming a solutions provider that engages directly with consumers to solve their challenges around nutrition, food and meal preparation, or bundling of products.

Look at your own strengths and how they could generate value in ways that others cannot match. Ask yourself:

- **What are the things we do uniquely well?** What are we recognized and admired for in the market? Why are we winning in the businesses in which we're strong? What are the differentiating capabilities that are at the heart of our success?

- **What else could these strengths enable us to do?** Could they be applied to solve additional big problems in the world? Could they be of use to our ecosystem partners?

This third lens could lead our food producer to leverage its highly efficient supply chain capability or to build on its unique freshness preservation technology.

By looking through these three lenses, you will most probably come up with quite a long list of ideas for how value could be created in your industry. Don't worry if you end up including what some may consider "crazy ideas"—you may even want to inject a few of those deliberately into the process in order to unconstrain your team's thinking and make sure you don't just end up with the usual suspects.

Step 2: Integrate Those Ideas into a Few Relevant Options for Your Place in the World

After you've widened the aperture in step 1 to generate ideas about how value can be created in your industry, now is the time to integrate these ideas into a few options for places in the world that are relevant for you.

What you're after is a value proposition that resonates with where you think the market is headed and that leverages your unique strengths. Relevant options typically aren't straightforward puretones—you will probably find that you need to combine a few puretones into a powerful value proposition that is truly differentiated. Relevant options don't just address a customer problem—they also allow you to tap into sizeable profit pools. And relevant options don't just address a market need—you must also be (or see a path toward becoming) uniquely good at addressing that need.

When you identify relevant options, make sure you set your level of ambition high. Don't feel constrained by the boundaries of your current value proposition or your current ability to deliver on it. Twenty-first-century ecosystems can accelerate your transformation because they allow you to collaborate more easily with other organizations and thereby provide bigger value to customers and gain access to the amazing capabilities that are required to get it done. Therefore, make sure that the options you are going to identify include a view of ecosystems and what they could enable you to do.

Our food producer might come up with three options: First, become a value player, focusing on a few key categories and using its scale-oriented supply chain capabilities to reduce cost and dominate the shopping aisle; second, become an innovator in plant-based food using its deep consumer insights and addressing people's desire for healthy eating and sustainability; third, become a healthy food solution provider, addressing people's desire for convenience and health.

Step 3: Make Your Bold Choice

Now that you've identified your most relevant place-in-the-world options, you're ready to assess them to determine which one gives you a right to win.[4] This involves considering two dimensions: market potential and your ability to bring something truly unique and differentiated.

At this point, you will want to chart out how your company would develop and thrive under each bold option, and how the market would evolve around you. Questions you need to address include:

- What would a company need to excel at creating value in the ways that correspond to each option? How does each option leverage our unique advantages?

- What differentiating capabilities would we need to build? Are we well-positioned to build or acquire those missing capabilities? Are there competitors or potential competitors that may be better-suited to thrive at this play?

- How would each option impact our portfolio? Would we need to divest some businesses and acquire others?

- How would each option impact how we work with and create value with our ecosystems?

- How would each option evolve in the market over time, and what would we need to do to shape our best possible future?

To answer that last question, in particular, we recommend running through some form of wargame to better understand how you would be positioned against today's or tomorrow's competitors, what moves could be particularly beneficial in establishing your place, and what could put you at risk. In such a strategic simulation, different teams put themselves into the shoes of various players (typically your company, customers, competitors, ecosystem partners, and regulators) and dynamically respond to each other's actions. By injecting shocks like changes in regulations or geopolitical turbulences into the wargame, you can identify whether externalities could make your place untenable. You will definitely want to know about those. But remember that, in most cases, making your place in the world successful is going to be up to you and how you face the market. Wargaming also gives you an opportunity to make the process creative, engaging, and fun. When you are seeking to define a fundamentally new future, you need to break the old model of strategic planning processes—where people are asked to fill in template after template, justifying why they think the market is going to grow by 3 percent versus 4 percent. Reimagining your company's place in the world requires that people bring their full creative potential, and a wargame can be particularly effective.

What if your team struggles to pick only one direction and wants to hedge your bets via multiple options? Remember that the goal must be to take all the creative energy and put most of it behind your new place—we call this *coherence*. Your value proposition, differentiated capabilities, and portfolio of products and services should all work together to give you the best shot at obtaining a right to win and to build the economic benefits of scale that come when your powerful capabilities are increasingly the center of everything you do. Some incoherence is natural—and even valuable if you launch experiments that allow you to learn from options you may not have pursued. But whatever incoherence you have, keep it small. Your leaders, organization, ecosystem, and most of all, your customers depend on you to deliver the value proposition you have promised.

In the end, you need to find a place that is relevant and unique and for which you are the rightful owner. Your stated place needs to be *relevant* to a set of customers or users with the potential to buy your products or services; it needs to be clear whose lives or businesses you are improving in some way, large or small. Your place must be *unique*—if you disappeared, you'd leave a hole in the marketplace. You must be the *rightful owner* of your stated place; you must have or be able to build the capabilities to excel at it and be able to do so more effectively and efficiently than your competitors.

Citigroup shows how to put these three steps into practice to fundamentally reimagine your place in the world and to keep updating it.

Citigroup: From Financial Supermarket to Focused, Digitized Bank

Citigroup ("Citi") began its corporate life as the City Bank of New York in 1812, and has played a starring role in the history of US banking—both the triumphs and the travails—ever since, from the Civil War through the Great Depression, through the deregulatory wave that began in the late twentieth century, through the financial crisis of 2007–2008 and the recession that followed. Citi has always innovated: It funded the first transatlantic cable in 1865 and was an ATM pioneer in the 1970s. By the 2000s, Citi had become a true financial supermarket, with a vast portfolio of operations in banking, brokerage, bond trading, insurance, and asset management that sought to offer all things financial to everyone, all over the world. The prevailing management style back then, recalls Michael Corbat, who spent his entire career at Citi and its predecessor companies and served as CEO from 2012 to February 2021, was acquisition-driven: "You'd go out, acquire a business, and then figure out what you were going to do with it. Then you'd move on, and eventually you'd do it again."

One business that Citi had acquired during its financial supermarket phase was subprime mortgage lending—the market that collapsed in 2007 and initiated the financial crisis. Citi came very close to being broken up or nationalized in the fall of 2008, before it was rescued—along with many other banks—with $45 billion in federal money in exchange for Citigroup equity. (Citi fully repaid the US government in December of 2009.) But the problem wasn't subprime mortgage lending only. Even before the crisis, Citi was drifting strategically, struggling to generate significant net income growth from its sheer scale in businesses and revenue.

The near failure was traumatic for the company's leaders, but it also provided a giant burning platform for transformation. Jane Fraser, the head of strategy when the financial crisis hit and now CEO of Citigroup, recalls one night in the fall of 2008 when the crisis was at its worst and Citi's failure seemed quite possible: "We thought the whole US financial system was going down, and when you have been through that, when you think everything has gone—all customer deposits, all savings in the system, and the rest of it—you have extraordinary clarity. You are remarkably indifferent to some of the decisions you have to make about your own institution. Every vested interest goes out the window."

"What the crisis really brought home to roost," continues Corbat, "was that we needed to redefine and restructure the company to create sustainability—sustainability in the eyes of our regulators, sustainability in the eyes of our customers and clients, sustainability in the eyes of our employees."

The soul-searching led to the conclusion that Citi needed to focus on the businesses where it had a right to win—it had to become smaller and more coherent to get stronger. The top team concluded that Citi needed to return to its roots. The first realization was that, at its core, Citi was and is a bank—not an insurance company, an asset manager, a hedge fund, or private equity firm. The second bet that leaders made was that Citi had to maintain and leverage its globality, one of Citi's unique advantages that is especially valuable for its multinational institutional clients who need a partner that can manage the complexity of transactions, currencies, and risk that result from the complexities of their own businesses. "Next," Corbat says, "we took those two axes—bank and globality—and said, 'What are the things that fit and what are the things that don't?' And it became obvious that there were a number of businesses that weren't necessarily bad businesses, but businesses that were not core to the future strategy." Leaders also wanted to ensure that Citi would be an aspirational, prime brand—which had remained true in some businesses and geographies, but not in others.

Citi's leaders created a subsidiary within the company's corporate structure to manage and divest the noncore assets—named Citi Holdings—with its own management team. Fraser remembers: "We were very clear that we needed to have two different entities. You cannot figure out how to best sell businesses in the morning and look at how to grow the core in the afternoon."

The scale of the transformation was huge. Through Holdings, Citi exited more than sixty operating businesses in more than forty countries that were deemed to be non-core—representing approximately $800 billion in assets and approximately one hundred thousand employees. "I don't think anything was ever attempted on this scale," says Corbat, who became CEO of Holdings in 2009. "$800 billion at the time—that was bigger than Morgan Stanley, bigger than Goldman Sachs, two times the size of GE Capital. And it was a third of our workforce that ultimately would need to leave the firm." On the institutional banking side, Citi went from thirty-two thousand clients to thirteen thousand; on the consumer side (where a global footprint was not as important for its value proposition as in commercial banking), Citi went from operating businesses in sixty countries before the crisis to nineteen as of the end of 2020.

With Citi now focused on its new place in the world—"a global bank that responsibly provides financial services that enable growth and economic progress for individuals and institutions," as the company puts it—it was ready to focus on organic growth in its targeted customer segments. Doing so required leadership to be focused and obsessed about service and creating value for customers. "We flipped the model," Corbat explains, "and went from being a product-centric organization to having a multi-relationship client approach—where the client is at the center rather than the products." The future Citi became more focused on the capabilities needed to improve the value that clients experience and how they experience it—including the products, services, and solutions it offered and the process of how clients would interact with the organization.

Citi invested heavily in technology and other enablers of its capabilities. It was clear that to be the best bank, it had to be the best digital bank. Says Corbat, "People talk about scale and the benefits of scale. But what scale? Is it your assets? Is it your deposits? Is it the number of branches? Is it the number of clients you have? Is it the number of countries? Probably yes, but I would actually put very high on that list technology and technology spend. Because today that's a true differentiator." Citi reportedly spends approximately 20 percent of its budget per year on technology and has added thousands of coders, data analysts, and other specialists (twenty-five hundred in 2020 alone in its trading and investment operations). It is also partnering with PayPal and Google to offer additional digital services—for example, a new digital checking and savings account with financial wellness and mobile functionality at the core of the design.

With everything they did, Corbat encouraged thinking "outside traditional banking," thinking about the broader things that are affecting people, and thinking about how Citi needs to offer its customers and clients solutions that match or exceed what he calls "best in life" experiences. "If that's their Uber experience or that's their Amazon experience—whatever that experience is—if you're not at least getting to that place, you have vulnerabilities," he says. "We need to own the responsibility of creating those best-in-life experiences. And oftentimes, that experience today is measured in how much friction we can take out of people's lives. Friction is time, friction is money, friction is aggravation. The expectation is that the good institutions will continue to remove those frictions, and provided that you can do that, I think you've got the ability to stay competitive." One service for which Citi has reduced friction is "streamlined documentation" and easy "digital onboarding," which enables customers to open accounts using electronic signatures—a service that was particularly valued during the Covid-19 pandemic.

Citi's transformation is ongoing with periodic refreshes. When asked about the main learnings from the Citi Holdings experience, Mark Mason, chief financial officer of Citigroup, stresses the discipline they've learned: "We're constantly looking at the portfolio and asking 'Does that make sense? Do I need to be in that? Is that a core competency that I have, and is it critical to the rest of my offering with clients?' The way we think about strategy is better informed because of what we've been through. There's probably a bit more of a willingness to carve off things that don't make strategic sense. After all, strategy is as much about what you do as it is about what you decide not to do."

This discipline also guides the transformation journey that Jane Fraser outlined in the early days of her tenure as CEO of Citigroup. She has reconfirmed Citigroup's place in the world as "the preeminent bank for clients with global needs in a digital world," and has initiated a strategy refresh that is guided by four principles:

- **Be clinical.** Assess in which businesses Citi can retain or secure leading market positions in a much more digitized world.

- **Be focused.** Direct investments and resources to the businesses that can drive stronger growth and improve returns over the long run, and away from those that cannot.

- **Be connected.** Ensure that businesses fit well together and capture the benefits of those linkages.

- **Be simpler.** Deliver a simpler firm to better serve clients, fulfill obligations to regulators, and unlock value for shareholders.

The strategy refresh has already led to a number of far-reaching decisions like doubling down on wealth management and exiting consumer businesses in thirteen markets across Asia, Europe, and the Middle East in which Citi does not have the scale to be successful.

Citigroup's transformation has been a brave one. It takes a lot of courage to cut back your organization so dramatically and to grow your business from this smaller, but stronger core. Citigroup got on this journey because it was facing an existential threat—and it has continued on this path to be one step ahead of where the world is going and shape its future. There is a lot more to do, as Jane Fraser pointed out when she took the CEO job on March 1, 2021, to address the serious issues raised by regulators and to improve the bank's returns. But consider this: after the near-death experience in 2008 and Citi's reimagination of its place in the world, Citi was named "World's Best Digital Bank" by *Global Finance* magazine in 2020. And the disciplines it learned back then are going to serve it well for the journey that's ahead.

. . .

Clearly defining your company's place in the world is key to your success beyond digital. Remember that the basis of competitive advantage has shifted to a world where you must be better than your competitors not just in the current set of products and services that go out the door every day, but in what you are able to do. Without rethinking the value you are creating for customers and end users and society at large, defining the differentiating capabilities you are going to scale up, and challenging the portfolio that you've assembled under the previous model of competitive dynamics, you won't be able to secure your company's future. Reimagining your place in the world today requires you to fundamentally question your company's reason for being and demands that you make big bets—even amid all the uncertainties about technologies, market structures, and economic and environmental conditions that keep business leaders awake at night.

As we've seen from the companies we've studied, and as you probably know from your own experiences, making such transformative choices can be daunting. But having seen these examples, we are also convinced that, once made, these bets provide a reassuring compass to help you take charge of your future and steer the journey.

3

Embrace and Create
Value via Ecosystems

I can do things you cannot. You can do things I cannot.
Together we can do great things.

—Mother Teresa

Japan's construction industry faces a fundamental problem: "one-third of the workforce is fifty-five and older, heading toward retirement, and younger people aren't taking jobs in construction anymore," says Tetsuji Ohashi, Komatsu's chairman of the board and former CEO. By 2025, according to a projection by the Japan Federation of Construction Contractors, there will be a shortage of some 1.3 million skilled construction workers. Meanwhile, the need is only increasing. "The social infrastructure—roads, bridges, and so forth—is deteriorating, and the many natural disasters we have in Japan, like floods or earthquakes, make the situation worse," Ohashi says.

In 2013, the year Ohashi became president, Komatsu first tried to address the industry's looming labor problems by introducing ICT (information, communications, and technology) construction machinery that used GPS, digital mapping, sensors, and IoT connections to enhance efficiency.

Those at Komatsu also realized that they needed to move much closer to their customers to gain better insights about the worksite issues they faced. That's why Ohashi concluded that they would leverage the rental business network that they had established since 2000, instead of selling off the machines, as they had done in their traditional "product-out" approach.

Based on these tighter connections to customers, Komatsu gained privileged insights that let leaders quickly see that the new machines were not resulting in the expected increase in productivity. The reason, they found, was bottlenecks in processes at the construction site both upstream and downstream from the process using their machines. At a highway construction site, for example, Komatsu's ICT machine could remove and dump 50 percent more dirt than a conventional machine, but construction companies were unable to schedule and account for the required number of dump trucks to remove the dirt from the site. Moreover, construction companies were unable to accurately forecast the volume of dirt they would be removing.

A Komatsu team analyzing the results found that the productivity of their machines only had an effect on a few of the many processes at a construction site. It became obvious that significantly increasing the productivity of construction sites could not be achieved by improving individual tasks performed by individual companies but would require a much higher level of coordination among all parties involved. That's why, in 2015, Ohashi created the SmartConstruction Promotion Division to work more closely with customers and other stakeholders involved in their construction projects. He named Chikashi Shike, who had overseen the team that led the construction site analysis, to head the division.

Shike remembers, "Mr. Ohashi asked us to look at things from the perspective of construction sites and all the parties involved in them—from order acceptance to completion. He said we had to go on with that in mind, even if that may not lead to the use of Komatsu construction machinery as a consequence." Smart Construction's mandate therefore was to move beyond selling, renting, and servicing machinery and to create solutions that would enable customers to shape safer and more productive construction sites.

The new solutions that went live just a few months later included high-resolution drone surveying and geographical data in 3D, a construction work planning tool, and tools for managing and using the 3D data uploaded to the cloud. It goes without saying that Komatsu wasn't able to develop all these solutions on its own. It accessed and integrated specific capabilities from many companies, including Propeller's capabilities in drone mapping and analytics; NVIDIA's experience in image processing, virtualization, and AI; Advantech's expertise with in-vehicle computing and communication; and Cesium's 3D geospatial technology.[1]

Komatsu worked hard to visualize all the elements of construction sites—machinery, dirt, building materials, and so on—along the entire construction process with 3D data, from field surveying, to design, preconstruction, construction, postconstruction inspections, upkeep, and maintenance. Komatsu could now connect all the people and companies involved in the construction and production tasks digitally. With so much now visible, companies across the ecosystem could collaborate to increase efficiency and productivity.

Beginning in 2017, Komatsu launched the open platform Landlog to further extend its efforts across the construction industry and enhance customer service. The Landlog platform, which can use information from other companies' machinery as well as Komatsu's smart construction information, has three major functions: visualizing construction processes, translating the data and images into actionable information, and providing application programming interfaces (APIs) that help users build their own applications against the Landlog platform to make construction sites smarter and safer. For instance, drones can complete a survey of a typical construction site in 20 minutes, down from three days, and Landlog can then integrate the data gathered by the drones to program automated bulldozers. Customers making their sites smart report being able to complete the construction job twice as quickly as they would otherwise, saving money and reducing pressure on overstretched construction workers.[2] Some 90 percent of Japan's construction companies have ten or fewer employees, with yearly sales of less than $600,000, so Komatsu is providing them with capabilities they could never have produced on their own, and Komatsu improves its own capabilities through having more data, more applications and greater leverage of its capability investments as the customer base grows.

Having started off by digitizing individual construction processes one-by-one (what Komatsu calls "vertical digitization"), the company has recently introduced new IoT devices and applications under the name "Smart Construction Digital Transformation" to digitize the entire process ("horizontal digitization"). This enables worksite operations to be optimized by synchronizing the real worksite with its digital twin, thereby realizing significant improvement in the safety, productivity, and environmental performance of the entire worksite. And as individual worksites are digitized, the next step will be the optimization of multiple worksites by connecting them remotely (which Komatsu calls "in-depth digitization").[3]

Shike says, "Komatsu is trying to shape its own future with a smart construction that leverages new open platforms, applications, and IoT devices. Previously, we were only involved in processes related to our own machinery, but that did not allow us to solve our customers' problems. We needed to involve many people, and because we needed a platform for people to be able to work together, we started Landlog. This in fact may change the structure of the industry."

By the end of 2020, Komatsu had introduced its Smart Construction to more than ten thousand construction worksites in Japan and has now also expanded the proposition to other countries, including the United States, United Kingdom, Germany, France, and Denmark. Aging of the construction workforce may be less of an issue in those countries, but the benefits in terms of safety and productivity of construction sites apply just as much.

Founded in 1921 as a manufacturer of industrial tools and construction equipment, this Japanese multinational corporation has experienced many ups and downs and changes in the hundred years since. However, the way Komatsu fundamentally rethought how it works and how it creates value for customers has let it shape its future and firmly taken it into the world beyond digital.

As your organization reimagines the place it will occupy in the changing business landscape, and as you build the differentiating capabilities you will deploy, you, too, will undoubtedly face many choices about how to tap into the game-changing opportunities that business ecosystems enable.

Why Ecosystems Matter

As we argued in chapter 2, your place in the world must be rooted in solving real customer or end-user problems. Many of today's unresolved problems, however, are so massive and complex that no single company can solve these issues by itself. Think about people's need for mobility, which requires dealing with public, shared, and privately owned methods of transportation, infrastructure, public 5G networks, energy supply, financing, regulation, and many more factors. Or about people's need for better health, which requires improving prevention, diagnosis, therapy, and post-therapeutic care. These problems can only be tackled by networks of companies and institutions that work together toward a common purpose. The sheer scale of the challenge and the investments required to address them almost always demands an ecosystem approach.

In addition, the era of expecting customers to be the synthesizers across their suppliers is over. Customers today expect that suppliers won't simply provide piece parts but will work together to deliver solutions of the sort that Komatsu orchestrated for construction companies with its ecosystem. Customers' expectations have risen steadily as they have faced increasing challenges and costs to combine resources from across multiple suppliers and partners. Suppliers must deal with a huge amount of complexity so that their customers don't have to—and customers will reward them.

Working with ecosystems is also vital for another reason: there simply isn't enough time or money to build the scale in capabilities that is required on your own. For example, in the beyond digital world, data is an essential currency to build deep customer insights that feed your value proposition (more on this in chapter 4), and you will have to reach outside your organization to access and build the scale in data you will need to gain those insights. Moreover, you need to scale your differentiating capabilities quickly, before someone beats you to it. You can't afford to fail because, for example, you couldn't find enough of the talent you need on time. Given that those individuals with deep expertise in a particular topic often prefer to work for organizations that specialize in that area and that can offer attractive career paths, you may need to access their skills via your ecosystem. What's more, with technology choices in particular often having long-term consequences, you may want to integrate some innovations from other companies rather than developing your own—helping you reduce the risk of obsolescence. Accessing capabilities from others in a trusted ecosystem can be a powerful way to quickly, reliably, and less expensively develop your source of differentiation. Make no mistake: You will absolutely own and build scale in some capabilities, and you'll be the integrator of all of this expertise and data, but be thoughtful about where you can truly differentiate. (See "The Nature of Modern Business Ecosystems.")

Philips's dramatic transformation, recounted in chapter 2, is an example of how a company developed a whole new range of business opportunities from ecosystems. As Philips refocused on

The Nature of Modern Business Ecosystems

The term *ecosystem* was first applied in a business context in a 1993 *Harvard Business Review* article by James F. Moore, a business strategist later known for his thought leadership in fields such as open technology, design thinking, and social change.[a] Moore described companies that were building new kinds of networks in the early days of the digital age. Previously, networks were tactical, typically limited to suppliers, distributors, sales channels, and a handful of other partners. Usually they were closed, members-only groups. They were often designed in a hub-and-spoke pattern, with most connections (and most of the value) going to the leader at the center of the network. They served mainly to improve the leader's costs and efficiency. Think about typical manufacturing outsourcing deals in the automotive or textile industries, for example.

The business ecosystems that evolved at the very end of the twentieth century and at the beginning of the twenty-first century, by contrast, are more strategic. In addition to realizing cost savings and efficiencies, in many cases ecosystem partners now collaborate on improving customer outcomes and creating new markets. These new ecosystems tend to involve more partners and a more diverse set of them. Usually, they operate with few formal rules and an ever-changing cast of participants. The connections are often many-to-many, not many-to-one.

A distinguishing feature of the new ecosystems is that the partners work together to maximize the *total* value. Instead of a twentieth-century outsourcing arrangement where an organization buys materials or services to improve its own production, the partners work together to achieve improved end-customer or

(continued)

user-oriented outcomes—creating a greater outcome that will compensate them all.

Four main flavors of ecosystems have developed: those built around a platform provider, an orchestrator, or an integrator, or innovation partnerships. The best-known are those with a platform provider at the center. This is the sort of ecosystem that Amazon has built, in which it connects buyers and sellers in a marketplace that it enables, or Facebook, where it enables users to connect via a social platform. An orchestrator-led ecosystem facilitates multiple participants to collaborate together to serve a broader objective with customers, where one player typically brings the fundamental aspects of the ecosystem together, coordinating activities but not bundling them together in one package. Komatsu is an example of an orchestrator. It allows multiple companies to share information on a common platform supporting construction projects so that customers can benefit; for instance, by providing transparency on the volume of material to be removed and coordinating excavators and dump trucks to minimize unproductive time. A third type, built around an integrator, assembles or curates related products and services into a bundled offering. This is what a hospital does by integrating various doctors, medical services, and clinics into a care system to serve patients. A fourth type, an innovation partnership, involves working across company lines to jointly develop breakthrough products. This is fairly common with automotive or aerospace companies, which work together across a vast ecosystem of suppliers and partners to develop products and solutions.

Fortunately, digital technology has lowered some of the hurdles to setting up and managing ecosystems. Broader, real-time connectivity means that those traditional hub-and-spoke networks can be reconfigured as many-to-many. In addition, it's easier to analyze and track the value that each partner is contributing and to have secure payment mechanisms. Potential concerns around trust have also been eased. There is more real-time transparency into what ecosystem partners are doing, which allows for earlier detection of bad behavior. There are also improved mechanisms to protect intellectual property via technologies such as blockchain. Of course, the challenges haven't gone away, but overall, it has become significantly easier to enter into and unwind partnerships.

a. James F. Moore, "Predators and Prey: A New Ecology of Competition," *Harvard Business Review*, May–June 1993, hbr.org/1993/05/predators-and-prey-a-new-ecology-of-competition.

providing better health outcomes, increasing efficiency, and improving the experience for patients as well as caregivers, leaders understood that these goals by their nature had to be pursued within the larger health-care ecosystem. As a result, Philips has built ecosystem partnerships with health systems, medical device companies, direct competitors, home care nursing providers, technology companies, and many others to deliver outcomes-based health-care services to its hospital customers. This ecosystem play has enabled Philips to establish, for example, its highly innovative fourteen-year strategic partnership with Karolinska University Hospital in Sweden, where the two organizations work together to transform the entire care life cycle for patients, including solutions like reducing the end-to-end "door to needle" time to save stroke patients who may be rushed into the hospital.[4]

Chief Innovation and Strategy Officer Jeroen Tas cites magnetic resonance imaging (MRI)—a field in which Philips was already a leading equipment provider—as an example of how the company leverages its ecosystem to deliver outcomes: "If we're not talking just MRI but are instead talking about getting more precise patient diagnoses, we may have to combine MRI, ultrasound, digital pathology, genomics, and a lot of other stuff that we don't make. We may need to interface with MRI machines that have been installed by our competitors. That means we have to rethink how we create those solutions, how we link to other people's modalities."

Microsoft CEO Satya Nadella says, "Partnering is too often seen as a zero-sum game—whatever is gained by one participant is lost by another. I don't see it that way. When done right, partnering grows the pie for everyone—for customers, yes, but also for each of the partners."[5] Under Nadella, Microsoft has refreshed its partnering spirit. Hundreds of thousands of companies around the world build and sell solutions that leverage Microsoft products and services. This greatly benefits Microsoft, which sees increased use of its products. But the connection also benefits its partners, which can build on Microsoft's strengths to develop solutions tailored to specific markets and needs. Customers benefit, too, because their very diverse needs and wants are better addressed than they could be by any single company.

Given the benefits that ecosystems enable and how accessible they've become, there isn't a way around them. Whether you decide to exploit ecosystem economics or not, your competitors will inevitably do so. No company that wants to thrive as the world goes beyond digital can ignore this reality. Creating value from within your four walls may have served you well in the past, but it won't do so going forward.

A powerful ecosystem play has the potential to change how an entire industry works. Look at our next example, a company that built an ecosystem of artisans making jewelry in India.

Titan: Redefining Its Future and the Future of Its Industry through a Wide-Ranging Ecosystem Play

Titan Company Limited is a natural ecosystem player, which has allowed it to transform India's jewelry industry, keeping alive the original art of the artisan while introducing modernity and scale.

Titan is the largest consumer company in the Tata Group—a conglomerate founded in 1868 that today has a sprawling portfolio of businesses ranging from software, automotive, steel, and chemicals to communications, consultancy, and consumer products. Titan was formed in 1984 under the name Titan Watches Limited and diversified in subsequent years into jewelry, eyewear, fragrances, accessories, and Indian dress wear (luxury saris). Titan expanded into jewelry in 1994 to capitalize on a fragmented market. At the time, the Indian jewelry business was highly localized, and the concept of branded jewelry was almost nonexistent. People typically bought from the same family jeweler their parents and grandparents had trusted, and most jewelry was made to order.

Titan's entry into the market wasn't easy. Says C K Venkataraman, managing director of Titan and former CEO of their jewelry business: "We are, in our heart, a manufacturing company, right from our beginning in watches. So rather than picking up jewelry from the local artisans and focusing on retailing, we set up our own manufacturing plant for jewelry." The company started offering designs that borrowed heavily from contemporary European brands, but they didn't resonate with local tastes.

After some difficult years, Titan took a step back and figured out how to offer more of what customers were used to buying—while adding unique value. Its leadership team concluded that they would have to shift from a manufacturing-centric company to an enabler of the existing ecosystem of local artisans and their customers, while using Titan's distinguishing capabilities to make the entire system better. The company set out to deliver artisanal quality and trust within a modern retail experience.

Says Venkataraman,

It's only when, around 2006–2007, we started reaching out more to local artisans—the *karigars*—that we realized how little the way they worked had changed over the past three hundred to four hundred years. It's difficult to imagine that the amazing jewelry they produce comes out of such dingy places: these are small rooms, with low ceilings, and temperatures can easily reach 40 to 45 degrees Celsius [104°–113°F] in summer. Karigars sit on the floor, with tube lights just above their heads lighting their work. They work on the floor, eat on the floor, take a siesta on the floor. It's completely unfair to artisans, and we recognized that unless we managed to materially change conditions for them, there was no way to make this model work. So we made it our mission to make it better for them—to "put the smile back on the karigar's face."

In 2014, Titan opened its first "Karigar center" for jewelry manufacturing at Hosur in Tamil Nadu.[6] The center houses three hundred artisans and provides dedicated workstations, comfortable accommodation, food in clean canteens, and an entertainment area. And Titan went further, building an ecosystem of eighty to ninety partners who employ some six thousand to seven thousand artisans across three hundred to four hundred locations. "For each of those partners and locations," says Venkataraman, "we have determined how they are doing along four dimensions: people, processes, place, and planet. Consider place, for example. We look at the tables at which the artisans work, the chairs on which they sit, the tools they use, etc. And for each of those four dimensions, we quantify their level of proficiency as cottage, basic, standard, or world-class. We have outlined a four-year journey for each one of those locations and vendor partners so that by 2023, they all reach 'standard' across any of the four dimensions." This program, while significantly improving the artisans' working conditions, also leads to an increase in quality; for example, when machines manufacture components that are more symmetric or precise than when made by hand.

Titan also improved the customer experience. While customer engagement had mainly taken place via the staff in Titan's more than four hundred retail stores across India, today digital channels play an essential role in understanding customer needs and tailoring offerings to individuals. Former Titan CEO Bhaskar Bhat adds, "Though not our largest investment, the most important investment we've made in the last few years is in analytics and customer relationship management. Our integrated loyalty program, Encircle, has a base of around eighteen million users in all our categories. By engaging with our customers digitally, we've been able to understand behavior and effectively translate that into more than a thousand targeted promotions."

Venkataraman says, "The karigar focus program is a huge and very exciting, very liberating kind of program for the jewelry division, because we keep alive the original art of the artisan, while at the same time introducing modernity." Titan's ecosystem play has paid off: its flagship brand, Tanishq, is India's leading jewelry brand; jewelry revenues doubled between 2014 and 2020, and profits grew 150 percent.

Let's now look at what steps you and your leadership team can take to determine what ecosystems to focus your attention on and how to play in them.

Making Your Ecosystem Strategy Work

The starting point in creating value via ecosystems is to take an inventory of the ones you already belong to. You're likely already part of many. Think about who the end users are for your products and services, then about who else is contributing to the larger goals where you're playing a role. Think about what other products, services, and capabilities could be available from other companies that could complement what you do and better serve your end users.

Then imagine what ecosystems you could be part of, even though you aren't at the moment. What new customers could you reach through partners? What important data could you gather? You will likely have considered some of these questions as you reimagined your place in the world, but this is your chance to continuously challenge and broaden how you participate in large customer and societal challenges.

It won't be easy. The leaders of the companies we researched did not always get their ecosystems right from the beginning. Sometimes they had to take a step back and correct something. But they highlighted a number of factors that have helped make their ecosystem strategies work. These can be grouped into four major themes:

- Shape your view on your ecosystem play—what role should you play in the ecosystem?

- Focus on the value you are creating for the ecosystem—not just what you're extracting from it.

- Clearly define what capabilities you contribute to, receive from, and deliver together with your ecosystem.

- Invest in building trust and deep understanding together with your partners.

Shape Your View on Your Ecosystem Play

As argued throughout this book, in the beyond digital age, your attention needs to shift from what you own to the value you are creating. This principle will also help you think through your ecosystem strategy. Let go of some things, perhaps including some of your data, to open new avenues. As long as you can measure the value you are creating through an ecosystem, what you own is less of a worry.

Consider whether you have what it takes to be an enabler of the ecosystem—whether a platform provider, an orchestrator, an integrator, or the organizer of an innovation partnership. You would need to excel at a range of capabilities, including development and management of a trusted platform, technological innovation, value management, partnership management, and trusted governance. And it would require significant investment and the fortitude to manage through high degrees of volatility. While much has been written about the virtue of companies becoming the next Amazon, Uber, or Airbnb of their ecosystems, remember that each of these companies had to survive through several nonprofitable years while sustaining huge levels of investment to secure the minimum scale needed to establish themselves as accepted platforms.

Platform providers, in particular, need to achieve significant network scale on the demand side, the supply side, or both. The scale of the network is a significant part of platforms' value proposition. For ride-sharing companies, for example, the more consumers use the platform, the more the platform can attract drivers; and the more drivers it has, the better the service for consumers. The most successful platforms enjoy this type of circular and reinforcing benefit. But when these benefits are smaller, suppliers and buyers may be compelled to join more than one platform (for example, many consumers and suppliers participate in several food delivery or entertainment platforms). Being clear about network effects and hurdles to join multiple platforms is critical if you are, or consider becoming, a platform provider.

Given the value of the network itself, some platform providers mistakenly assume it is enough to give them a sustained competitive advantage. Not investing enough in creating meaningful differentiation beyond the network, however, is risky: you set yourself up to lose your position either because another player adds meaningful differentiation or because governments intervene to prevent your network from getting too large.

To succeed as a platform provider (and more generally as an enabler) over time, you need to continue to invest and improve your value proposition to stay ahead and keep the network loyal. Amazon, for instance, not only pioneered one-click buying but then made a massive investment in Prime, which began by offering free two-day shipping—making Prime members, who now number 150 million in the United States, much more likely to buy from Amazon. The company continues to add features to Prime, including entertainment, to lock in customers and discourage competitors from even trying to match it. And its ongoing massive investments in its supply chain are making it increasingly difficult for others to compete in a world where low-price reliable delivery is key.

Being an enabler could be the right choice for you—as a platform provider, an orchestrator, an integrator, or the organizer of an innovation partnership. But there are other ways to play that can create value far beyond what can be achieved alone—as a participant in one or many parts of multiple ecosystems. Says Stewart McCrone, Philips's head of strategy, M&A, and partnerships, "You have to stop considering yourselves as the center of the universe. Where necessary, you have to put yourself into a subsidiary role. We can be number two or number three in a perfectly gold-mine ecosystem, and we will take our share of the spoils. It's difficult to mentally make the shift to do that, but I'm pushing my team to constantly think more about what the ecosystem is, where it is going, and how we can play. And we might play in the lead, or we might not."

It's often easier to get started as a participant, because the reduced friction in commerce in the beyond digital era makes it simpler to connect with others and plug into an ecosystem. Participants typically provide data, customer access, intellectual property, or a part of a value chain. But the demands for differentiation are even greater for participants than for an enabler—the fact that you can easily plug in to an ecosystem means that a competitor can as well, impacting both your share of and your importance to the rest of the ecosystem. You also have to make sure that you pick a winning ecosystem because even if you play your part right, you still lose if another eco-system bests yours. And you must be careful about the intentions of the ecosystem partners and the enabler.

Your role may also evolve. Komatsu did not plan from the start to develop the Landlog platform that would allow it to orchestrate its ecosystem. Leadership only decided to step up and turn the company into an ecosystem enabler, on top of its participant role, once they found that otherwise, they wouldn't be able to improve their custom-ers' construction site efficiency as much as desired.

Focus on the Value You're Creating for the Ecosystem—Not Just What You're Extracting from It

If the ecosystem thrives, everyone is going to benefit. If individual members are only interested in what they're getting out of the eco-system, it is going to fall apart.

You need to look at how you can symbiotically increase value with your ecosystem partners. Your value proposition must help increase the value of the ecosystem, and the ecosystem must in turn help you expand the value you can create. Without this collaboration, you have nothing more than a slightly better traditional partnership or customer-vendor relationship, which may be valuable but will most likely not help you create truly differentiated value.

Titan could have attempted to have artisans compete against each other on price and improved its margins—but that would have led to further deterioration of the artisans' conditions and sapped their interest in the ecosystem. Titan's leaders did the contrary. They rec-ognized that they needed to materially improve conditions for kari-gars or there was no way to make the model work—not now and not in the future, when the artisans' children and grandchildren would choose a different trade. Instead, Titan established a symbiotic rela-tionship with its ecosystem. The company accessed the great artisanal skills of the karigars, which allowed it to sell jewelry that resonated with consumers' diverse local tastes. Karigars' working conditions greatly improved, and their creations got into the hands of customers beyond the village in which they were based. Customers could buy trusted quality jewelry of artisanal style across all of India while enjoying a modern retail experience. Titan, the karigars, and customers all got better value through this ecosystem play.

Ecosystems work when everyone wins. You have to measure what you're gaining *and* what you're contributing.

Clearly Define What Capabilities You Contribute to, Receive from, and Deliver Together with Your Ecosystem

As argued before, one of the key benefits of modern ecosystems is that they let you access partners' capabilities at speed, at scale, and in a flexible way. In order to thrive in this new world, you will therefore need to reassess what you do, what your partners do, and where you combine forces to build the differentiating capabilities that are required. This will most probably significantly shift the boundaries of your organization.

Start by determining what is key for creating your place in the world and bringing the value to your ecosystem(s) that you promised to deliver. That's what you should spend the bulk of your energy on. For everything else, there may well be someone in the ecosystem that's better positioned to deliver the capability, be it because the activity is closer to the core of their purpose, because they've built more scale than you have, or for other reasons.

As to the capabilities that are at the heart of your value propositions, while you will need to deliver the ultimate outcome of that capability, you don't necessarily need to develop every bit of it in-house—you may as well combine forces with the ecosystem. Ask yourself:

- What bits (e.g., a given technology) are missing that would need to be integrated to make those capabilities world-class?

- Is there someone in our ecosystem who could help us fill those gaps in a way that does not put our differentiation at risk? Would they be faster, better, cheaper than we are?

- Is that an area to which we don't want to fully commit because the future is too uncertain? Should we share that risk with a partner?

Thinking through those questions will help you assess what you should do versus in which areas you should partner. The right model may well shift over time as your level of proficiency improves and what's required to succeed change.

Invest in Building Trust and Deep Understanding Together with Your Partners

To make your ecosystem play work, you need to really understand what matters to your ecosystem partners, build trust with your ecosystem, and invest in managing the change.

Deeply understand what matters to your ecosystem partners. To create value together, you need to understand what motivates your ecosystem partners, how they work, how they think, what their DNA is like, and how what you do really adds value to them. You can't collaborate effectively with someone you don't understand.

We are not referring to cosmetic efforts to understand one another, such as joint social events and annual kickoff meetings. While these tactics have their place, successful ecosystem relationships require real investment in the form of time spent working together, without necessarily achieving an immediate result. As part of its renewed partnership spirit, Microsoft has put in place a One Commercial Partner unit focused on better understanding the needs of its partners, simplifying the engagement between partners and Microsoft's own sales organization, and enabling partners to effectively serve customers. Some companies even decide to share office space and co-locate for stretches simply to build a real understanding that goes beyond the superficial.

Really understanding your ecosystem partners takes time and effort. They may be from a different industry that has much stricter or looser regulations or that moves at a very different speed than what you are used to. They may be much smaller or much larger than you are. They may have more or less experience working in an ecosystem setting. It won't be easy to understand what they need and why they operate the way they do. But without this deep understanding of your ecosystem partners, you simply won't be able to generate the type of value required in the beyond digital age.

Build trust with your ecosystem. The different players need to trust one another not only to play by the rules of the ecosystem but also to remain true to the intent of the relationships. Ecosystem plays can often take time (sometimes many years) to nurture the right relationships to build the levels of trust and understanding required. This is why some of the most obvious areas where companies like Philips began developing ecosystem-based value-creation models were with partners and customers with whom they had well-established relationships. Ecosystem plays may also require significant commitments of leadership, political, and financial capital from each of the participants to establish the required trust.

Make sure to invest in ways to objectively measure performance and ensure trust. Today, several ecosystems use technology like secure blockchain tokens to ensure trusted transactions within the ecosystem. Others use unbiased third parties to audit and ensure trust in the relationship. Whatever approach you choose, establish mechanisms that build and sustain trust for the health of the ecosystem.

Invest in change management. Many leaders have grown accustomed to outsourcing some of their back-office processes, but ecosystems are a very different animal. They are not about reducing cost by a few percent; they are about maximizing value for customers. Ecosystems are not about squeezing suppliers' margins but about establishing strategic partnerships where you can only win if your partners are well off. Ecosystems do not represent an incremental change but a massive shift in the boundaries of your organization and in how leaders need to lead.

In the past, ecosystem management or partnership management was often relegated to some business development group or a government relations department. Now, your whole organization needs to be much more externally aware, sensing, connected.

Years of organizational DNA, processes, and systems encouraging employees to define value in an insular way and/or ideas of beating the competition may need to be rewired. How can you have your organization learn to first look outside, not inside, for new ways of creating value? How can you have your employees look beyond doing everything in-house and think more broadly to see what value can be created by partnering with others? How do you make decisions about what should be done in-house versus externally? How do you choose where to compete versus collaborate? Making these decisions will require implementing clearly defined processes across every function within the organization. All functions and all levels will need to be aware of ecosystem thinking and understand where it matters and where it doesn't. The clarity you have achieved when defining your place in the world and your role in the ecosystem will help make sure that not every part of the organization pursues its own, disconnected ecosystem strategy.

Such a fundamental rewiring of the organization cannot be easily achieved overnight. It requires you to carefully plan the transition. What functions do you start with? Which ecosystem partners do you first bring on board? Most importantly, you must engage your people on an individual basis to help them think about value differently and learn to collaborate in new ways.

Cleveland Clinic: Expanding Its Reach and Further Improving Care through Its Ecosystem Play

Let's look at another example. With revenues of $10.6 billion in 2020, and 19 hospitals and more than 220 outpatient locations worldwide, Cleveland Clinic is one of the world's most admired health care systems. The company employs more than seventy thousand caregivers, who conduct more than eight million patient visits annually. Founded in 1921, the health care system has built distinctive capabilities in patient-centric care, translational research (bringing new approaches from the laboratory to the bedside), and continuing education of doctors, nurses, and other personnel to create better care and patient experiences. With many medical firsts in the United States, such as performing a coronary angiography (1958), larynx transplant (1998), near-total face transplant (2008), transcatheter valve replacement and repair (2011), and robotic single-port kidney transplant (2019), Cleveland Clinic is ranked the number two hospital in the world by *Newsweek* and has been ranked number one in cardiology and heart surgery in the United States by *U.S. News & World Report* for twenty-six straight years. It has also been a leader in digital health, pioneering electronic medical records, telehealth, and the use of machine learning and AI to analyze health data.

Yet despite its stellar successes, Cleveland Clinic was limited to being a local health care system tethered to where it had physical infrastructure and could actually receive patients. While technology allows for some sharing of knowledge, it didn't solve how to extend Cleveland Clinic's differentiated capabilities in health-care services more tangibly and meaningfully across multiple locations—not until

Cleveland Clinic adopted its version of the ecosystem play. As one step in that journey (other steps include the expansion across Ohio, to Nevada and Florida, to Canada, and most recently the UK), in 2006, it announced an ecosystem partnership with Mubadala Development Company to develop Cleveland Clinic Abu Dhabi (CCAD), a state-of-the-art, 364-bed specialty hospital. Working together, both organizations would expand access to Cleveland Clinic's groundbreaking and differentiated capabilities by replicating the Clinic's unique DNA, while using their ecosystem partner's capabilities to inject innovation and insights and move faster.

This partnership was critically important for both Cleveland Clinic and Mubadala, the United Arab Emirates–owned sovereign wealth fund. For Cleveland Clinic it was a way to expand its reach to patients far from home and live up to its ambition to care for all who need it. For Mubadala, this partnership was an important step toward realizing the government's Economic Vision 2030 to develop a robust, world-class health-care sector to address a range of unique and complex care requirements of Abu Dhabi's population, reducing the need for patients to travel abroad for treatment. Besides having developed the vision to provide Western health care to the Emirates and contributing monetary resources, Mubadala would inject its expertise in navigating local processes and regulations, integrating the new hospital into the local health-care system, managing such a complex partnership, financial management, and bring its breakthrough thinking to generally push the limits of what was considered feasible.

Tom Mihaljevic, MD, who joined the company as a cardiac surgeon in 2004 and now is Cleveland Clinic's CEO and president, was appointed CEO of the new Abu Dhabi facility in 2015 with a mission to imprint Cleveland Clinic's DNA into the new venture. "Abu Dhabi was our first attempt to replicate the quality of our organization's structure, as well as the quality and experience of care, in a location distant from the main campus where our journey started," says Mihaljevic, "and we demonstrated that we could deliver the excellence of US health care outside North America. This is something that in our industry has never been done before. Cleveland Clinic Abu Dhabi is now widely recognized as the best hospital in the Middle East. And the reason why we succeeded is because we firmly committed to replicate our system."

Being able to expand Cleveland Clinic's impact to a broader healthcare ecosystem was already highly rewarding. But the CCAD partnership also unexpectedly enriched Cleveland Clinic's systemwide practices and capabilities. "The reverse learning happens continuously," says Mihaljevic, who came back from his post in Abu Dhabi to be CEO and president of the global organization in 2018. "The lessons we learned over there have influenced every aspect of our current functionality across the system in the United States as well as in our new ventures. We have almost jokingly come to the conclusion that we should do a large-scale greenfield project every four to five years because it's a real opportunity to accelerate our learnings, that we then extrapolate across the system."

One example of reverse learning from CCAD is in digital tools. "The goal was to make Cleveland Clinic Abu Dhabi the most digitally enabled hospital in the world," says Mihaljevic. "Since we were starting from scratch, we were able to do things there that we weren't doing anywhere else and leverage those throughout the system, like our new electronic medical records or a new patient-friendly mobile app for navigating the hospital."

One example of a highly critical and differentiated process was the implementation of "tiered daily huddles," which are structured, fifteen-minute meetings each morning where team members discuss significant issues such as any safety and quality concerns, the number of patients in the hospital, and the number awaiting entry. The tiers start with the frontline units within the hospital and continue up the hierarchy to the executive leadership—providing leaders daily performance data on quality, patient safety, and access. Mihaljevic instituted the practice in Abu Dhabi to make sure he had a pulse on everything that was happening. It has now been adopted throughout Cleveland Clinic's global operations and has dramatically improved the quality and safety of the care because it mobilizes teams to address their performance every day. (For more on tiered daily huddles and how they drive engagement across the organization, see chapter 7.)

Cleveland Clinic's approach to learning from various parts of the ecosystem is the opposite of "not invented here." "We figure out some new application of digital in Abu Dhabi, and then use it here in the main campus. We're doing something breakthrough in heart surgery in the main campus and then apply it in Abu Dhabi. And we're going to take all of this to London and learn what we can," says James Young, MD, former chief academic officer of Cleveland Clinic, now executive director of Academic Affairs. "Multilateral learning and multilateral relationships do make a health-care system like ours go." Today, Cleveland Clinic shares and scales innovations across the ecosystem—from London to Abu Dhabi, or Abu Dhabi to Cleveland—to make the entire system better.

On a more strategic level, the success of the CCAD venture has given Cleveland Clinic the confidence that it can authentically replicate the quality of care it provides and that this ecosystem play is the right mechanism to further expand their services to places far away from the main campus. "It showed us there is not something that is magical and that can grow only in Northeast Ohio," says Mihaljevic. "We would not have embarked on Cleveland Clinic London [a 205-bed facility near Buckingham Palace due to open in 2022] had we not been encouraged by our success in Abu Dhabi." CCAD taught Cleveland Clinic important lessons about how to create value through ecosystems: "We learned that even in different models, without that complete control, we can have a significant impact," says Josette Beran, former chief strategy officer. "Working with our partner, we learned a lot about rigor, business, how other organizations work, and around effective governance and delegation of authority. We also learned a lot about how to work with other cultures: understanding the cultural nuances and sensitivities, appreciating that there are differences, and knowing how to interact."

This innovative project led to incorporating other ecosystem partners and suppliers to push the boundaries of how Cleveland Clinic delivers health care, including the expansion to London.

Another breakthrough ecosystem play was announced in early 2021 around the Global Center for Pathogen Research & Human Health, where Cleveland Clinic is combining forces with the state of Ohio and IBM to prepare and protect the world against future public health threats like the one from Covid-19. Headquartered in Cleveland and spanning the Clinic's international footprint, the Center will bring together a world-class research team and several research centers to broaden understanding of viral pathogens. IBM will bring to bear its quantum computing, cloud, and artificial intelligence capabilities to help speed research into viruses and genomics. The state of Ohio sees the Center as a significant economic catalyst in northeast Ohio, generating an estimated 1,000 jobs at Cleveland Clinic by 2029 and an additional 7,500 jobs in Ohio by 2034.

Through the successful set up of the hospital in Abu Dhabi, Cleveland Clinic has proven the ability to extend its differentiated capabilities to break the chains restricting hospital providers into only specific locations and health care systems and extend their impact globally. The new hospital has also given Cleveland Clinic the confidence to take a much more proactive role in shaping its ecosystems and extending them into new areas like research. "In the past, when a company approached us about a partnership, we would talk about it and figure out what to do," says James Merlino, MD, Chief Clinical Transformation Officer. "But we've now shifted the mindset to 'what do we want to achieve and whom do we need to partner with to get there?'"

. . .

In the beyond digital age, companies need to work together in ecosystems to solve the big problems that matter to customers and society. Assembling the right ecosystem and working productively with it isn't easy. But we hope that the examples in this chapter inspire you to embrace ecosystems more wholeheartedly and provide useful guidance into how to make your ecosystem strategy work.

4

Build a System of Privileged Insights with Your Customers

Nothing is more terrible than activity without insight.

—Thomas Carlyle, Scottish historian and essayist

Companies spend billions of dollars every year to gain information about their customers, buying data from market research firms, running study after study, and using big data and sophisticated analytical models to make sense of it all. Yet few leadership teams can say they have *unique* data about their customers, and even fewer have unique and relevant *insights* about what customers need and want. But having such unique insights is essential for a business to stand out from the competition as the world moves beyond digital.

Privileged insights is the term we use for the kind of customer understanding that is critical in today's marketplace. Privileged insights are unique to your organization—and often uniquely valuable to you—and are developed from a combination of data, experience, and relationships that your competitors don't have. (See "The Data and Technology Imperative.") These insights provide powerful ammunition to differentiate your organization from other players and to develop products, services, and solutions that are relevant in the market despite the sea changes around you. If done right—as part of your normal course of business—your activities to gain insights improve the customer experience and reinforce the value you're offering. Think about how Apple's Genius Bar helps users get the most out of their devices *and* is a place where customers share some of their most important digital challenges directly with the company.

The greater the engagement with customers, the more you learn; the more you learn, the more you improve the value proposition; the more you improve the value proposition, the more trust you generate (by delivering on your promise), and the more you gain engagement and an opportunity to learn.

Our research into Adobe provides a powerful, extended example of how privileged insights can be developed and can let leaders see much further along their value chains to gain unprecedented understanding of how to best serve customers. The San Jose–based software company had made a successful change in 2014, away from selling its widely used applications (like Photoshop, Illustrator, and InDesign) as packaged products, mostly as CDs via third-party sellers. Instead, Adobe began to offer the applications as cloud-based, software-as-a-service (SaaS) solutions via direct subscription. In 2014, 50 percent of revenue came from subscriptions; in 2016, the subscription share was 78 percent. The impact to topline growth following the changeover was equally solid—from over $4 billion in 2014 to nearly $6 billion in 2016.

But Adobe's move to the cloud, though successful, is not the main story we want to focus on here—rather, we investigate how the company reconfigured its operating model around the data and consumer insights that it was now able to use, and how that supercharged its business.

Leaders indeed felt that there was plenty of room to accelerate the company's growth, and that improving awareness of what their customers needed would let them better shape Adobe's future. "We were at an inflection point for our business," says Ashley Still, senior vice president and general manager for Digital Media. "We were following market growth rates and growing with our user base, but we were having difficulty accelerating that growth rate."

Before the move to cloud-based software and subscription-based sales, Adobe marketers knew very little about their users. Since its products were sold mostly through third parties and the apps were largely used offline, all Adobe knew was basically when a customer registered a product. Moving to SaaS, however, gave the company the ability to see how customers were *using* its applications in real time and to identify both opportunities and pain points continuously by analyzing the millions of data points it was able to capture. Adobe then set out to make full use of the opportunity the new model offered, by essentially reorienting much of its value creation model—and organizational structure, as a logical next step—around customer insights.

"We aspired to have a direct relationship with customers in ways that we had never had before, which was a significant strategic pivot," says Still. "With just a few customers, we could watch their entire experience and journey with Adobe by simply looking over their shoulder—but with millions of customers, having a direct relationship with every one of them would be impossible at scale. We knew we couldn't do it directly with our own sales team, nor through our partners."

Adobe's leaders concluded that they could overcome the scaling challenge and create winning customer experiences by using data and digital instrumentation. That's when the company began to put in place what they now call their data-driven operating model (DDOM, as it's referred to internally). Adobe launched a company-wide transformation to unify data architectures across the organization that would allow it to capture and analyze customer insights in new, robust, and scalable ways.

Cynthia Stoddard, senior vice president and CIO of Adobe, explains: "Like most companies, we used to have data silos; people had their own datasets and reported out of that dataset. And there was a lot of trying to figure out why numbers didn't match." DDOM oriented all of Adobe's data around the five steps of the journey a customer experiences with an Adobe application: Discover, Try, Buy, Use, and Renew. For each of the five steps, the company would define key metrics; for example, organic traffic (in Discover), unqualified to qualified conversion (in Try), conversion (in Buy), week 4 return rate (in Use), or user-initiated cancel rate (in Renew). And the company redeployed work teams around these steps: each of the five steps has a VP-level "metrics owner" and the weekly meetings to review KPI progress are attended by more than one hundred people, sometimes including C-level executives.

Eric Cox, vice president of Digital Media GTM & Sales in the Americas, describes how this new level of customer insight gained through DDOM changed how Adobe operated: "This model fundamentally shifted how we operated by creating a common language around data. From individual contributors to the C-suite, any decision that impacted the overall customer experience had to be made with insights and not purely intuition or educated guesswork."[1] He gives an example: "For some time, a great deal of resources (and mindshare) had been focused on a few specific mobile apps that we had instinctively felt were priorities for the company. What DDOM revealed to us—through the new KPIs that focused on user journeys—was that some neglected apps were actually driving tremendous value for our customers. It pushed our teams to divert resources and deliver new onboarding experiences. These efforts have since driven significant engagement and conversion for Adobe's overall mobile offerings."

Adobe CFO John Murphy says, "DDOM was a game changer for us. We started with the aspiration to measure fifty-three customer journey KPIs, but quickly found that we could go deeper into the customer journey to find more insights and ways to better serve our customers. Today, DDOM scales across hundreds of KPIs and is instrumental in helping highlight the insights that matter most, creating a much more dynamic experience."

Take, for example, an individual consumer who's purchased Photoshop. Murphy notes that it's a complex product with many powerful capabilities and that some users may find it overwhelming, leading them to stop using the app—and, eventually, to cancel their subscriptions. "What we're able to see, and evolve through artificial intelligence," says Murphy, "enables us to anticipate what someone is trying to do." If a person is becoming frustrated while editing a photo, for example, Adobe can detect their problem based on which menus they are accessing and what they're clicking on. This goes well beyond the kind of generic messages that pop up on many websites and programs, asking whether there's something they can help you with. "In the app itself," says Murphy, "they'll get a message saying 'Hey, I think you're trying to apply this filter,' and it will enable them to fix the issue with a single click or click on a tutorial that'll show more detail about how to solve their problem. We've been enhancing our capability for creating that kind of engagement for years."

DDOM has quickly picked up speed internally. "Starting small, with just a few metrics, was really important," Stoddard explains. "It allowed us to show the value of having that one set of metrics, of having that unified data architecture, and managing the business in this data- and insights-driven way. So, we had people come knocking at our door saying, 'We want to be part of this.'"

Adobe's success with DDOM led the company to launch the Adobe Experience Platform in early 2019, to sell its insights system to other companies. "We 'productized' our data-driven operating model for other enterprises," says Murphy, "so that they could create that same journey for their customers and gather data that's relevant for them, that's very domain-specific to them. The Adobe Experience Platform allows other companies to leverage our experiences when they rethink how they engage with their customers. It was a really transformative event for the company."

Adobe's ability to know what their millions of customers like and don't like about their experience with Adobe's offerings as they move through the customer journey informs all the company's choices about its marketing messages, customer experience, or product features. Adobe's leaders credit most of the company's revenue growth from $5.9 billion in 2016 to $12.9 billion in 2020 to their data-driven insights capability. As the company states: "We've come a long way, moving from a distant, intermittent relationship with our customers to a 24/7, personalized interaction. As a result, we've consistently reaped the benefits—including happier, more engaged customers, greater recurring revenue, and much more."[2]

Like many other software companies, Adobe went from selling boxed software to selling SaaS. But, unlike most others, it took full advantage of this move, building a privileged insights system that allowed the company to grow much more rapidly than they could have done otherwise. The privileged insights not only grew Adobe's traditional business but also opened a new stream of revenue from selling the DDOM capability to other companies, an example of how ecosystems have shifted to strongly value the capabilities an individual player can provide.

Gaining Privileged Insights—a Key Capability

Businesses have always needed to know their customers, but in the world beyond digital, the need for insights—privileged insights—is even more acute. Companies win because they're able to address a fundamental need of their customers better than anyone else. What that exact need is, however, evolves over time; and what it takes to excel at addressing the need changes all the time, in ever-faster inno-

The Data and Technology Imperative

As you go beyond digital, you will need to make sure you address the underlying data and technology needed to support your differentiating capabilities, including your privileged insights system. Your differentiating capabilities will need to be fed by privileged insights, which in turn will need to be fed by data, and that data will need to be supported by the right technology to capture it and create insight. In short, you will struggle to succeed with capabilities-based differentiation without a data and technology strategy that supports it. Too many companies don't have a proper data and technology strategy clearly linked to their value creation strategy. Instead, too often, data and technology investments are siloed. To go beyond digital, you will need to make a priority of your data and technology strategy and how it supports your corporate strategy.

In many ways, data has become a new super-currency. The data you have—not just in your customer relationship management (CRM) systems, but also in your finance systems in the form of billing data, in your supply chain and logistics systems in the form of insights on your lead times, with your ecosystem partners and even perhaps with your third-party sellers—can provide incredible insights to help you create value. Every interaction with customers, every moving part in your supply chain, every financial transaction, and a host of other activities your business performs have the potential to help you improve customer insights, build products faster, spot fraud, react to events before they happen, stop customer churn, and even prevent accidents. And of course, that data can also help you drive business innovation and open up new revenue streams.

(continued)

The data you need does not have to come from within the four walls of your organization. In fact, the data within your organization is likely to be insufficient. This is especially so given the use of AI models that require vast amounts of data so that algorithms can be tested to make accurate predictions. The more data you have, the more holistic it is, and the fresher or closer to real time it is—the better your predictions and the more solid your insights are likely to be. And given the increasingly frictionless nature of the business environment (see chapter 3 on ecosystems) and the relative ease of exchanging data, you don't necessarily need to *own* all that data. While you will want to protect some of your most privileged data, you can create scale in your data assets by tapping into the information that other companies have built in many other areas. Leading companies now are more willing to source and share data—because sharing information (securely and consistent with your privacy policies) allows them to also receive data in return. That is why Komatsu collects on its Landlog platform data from all companies involved on a construction site—and shares it with everyone involved so companies can better coordinate and avoid bottlenecks.

What this means is that companies need to develop and drive a multifaceted data agenda that includes both a defensive posture— securing the data they have as an asset—and an offensive one— seeking data as an investment. They need to define how they explore, collect and store data; develop and enforce clear governance that specifies quality, format, and method of data provision in line with privacy and security needs; invest in and apply the highest standards in terms of cybersecurity; build a data analytics capability by making big decisions about and investing in the right tools, technology, talent, and culture; develop and manage the ecosystems with which they are sharing data; and discover business opportunities through internal and external data analysis and sharing. In short, companies have a lot to do.

How you address data therefore requires a strategic approach and leadership attention. It requires focus and real investment to make the right choices about how you build your data management maturity and capabilities, and how you feed this into the range of your business needs for insight—whether for internal process improvements or to enable more relevant value propositions and new products and solutions. It is for this reason that a number of companies have gone so far as to appoint a chief data officer (CDO) empowered to fully focus on driving the company's data agenda with a seat at the top team table. While there are many organizational solutions that might work for your situation, having leadership engagement is not only an action for those companies, it is for all companies that go beyond digital and use data in ways that create new value. Your data strategy needs to become a key part of your corporate strategy. And your data strategy and corporate strategy cannot stand alone—they have to be supported by your technology strategy and priorities.

The technology that helps companies capture data and turn it into insights exists and continues to quickly be innovated. Cloud-based enterprise resource planning (ERP) solutions, on-demand storage, connected sensors, machine learning and AI tools, and many other technologies to collect, process, and analyze data rapidly, flexibly, and creatively abound. There's a wide array of options available.

These technology investments, however, can be challenging for two primary reasons: (1) the sheer size of investment that is often needed, and (2) the uncertainty of the potential payoff. Turning off legacy systems and converting to new technologies can be very

(continued)

expensive. And given the difficulty of getting people to adopt and use the new systems, securing a reasonable return on investment can be very challenging. It is difficult, for example, for data scientists to commit up front that the AI algorithms they build will reliably work and can deliver a bankable savings or revenue number as payback within a specified time. Their work requires trial and error that comes as part and parcel of the technology.

Companies today therefore need a strong perspective about which technologies to innovate and build versus leverage and integrate from their ecosystems. We recommend shaping your technology and data priorities, using your place in the world and privileged insights as a guide. Should you invest in back-office systems or in a front-end customer engagement platform? Should you look to improve the quality of your finance data or your supply chain data? The business cases for these investments should be based on whether they help contribute to building the differentiating capabilities that are key for securing your place in the world. And your privileged insights can help guide which investments will help you earn a differentiated place with your customers. As you consider how you shape your technology agenda, we offer some questions that may help you prioritize what is right for your company:

- Is the technology investment contributing to the heart of your differentiating capabilities, or is it supporting other needs?

- Is it supporting you in building for tomorrow or securing today? What impact will the investment have on your company's place in the world?

- Can you acquire and retain the talent critical to developing that technology and making it relevant for your business? Is it essential to your differentiating capabilities to build the talent base within your organization?

- Does the technology capability you need already exist somewhere in your ecosystem or in the broader supplier market? Can you tap into it while at the same time protecting your differentiating capabilities and not putting your competitive advantage at risk?

- Can you build reliable partnerships and relationships to execute with a balance of speed and efficiency?

- Are all the stakeholders who need to change in order to realize the value of your technology investments committed? Can they be held accountable? Do you have the governance model in place to ensure and enforce individual and collaborative accountability?

- Is your organization and culture ready for change? Can you ensure that your people can incorporate the technology you build?

This is a starter list and certainly not exhaustive. However, working through these questions can help you address the success factors to shape the data and technology strategy that will support your beyond digital vision.

vation cycles. Having good customer insights isn't good enough, because others can get them as well. Instead, you have to assiduously invest in gaining privileged insights to fuel your competitive differentiation.

While you may already engage directly with customers, you may not have the systems or tools to drive the type of output required from that engagement. The good news is that advances in technology that provide elements of what you need are becoming the norm, as are companies that will provide you with those elements. For example:

- In the capture of data, new tools and technologies allow for more granular and valuable information about customers along the entire customer interaction cycle. In retail stores, cameras in the ceilings can watch how (anonymized) customers make their way around, see which items they linger over but don't buy, pick up and put back on the shelf, and more. And, of course, such tracking can be done as customers peruse information on websites. IoT devices can, with customers' permission, provide data on how a product is used and how it performs, as do customers' online comments and ratings. Other exchanges with customers (call centers, warranty support, financing, follow-up services) can be used to build in questions that support understanding customers' needs and can now be digitized for analysis. Technology also provides information on social habits that can offer insight into purchase decisions.

- In the analysis of information, AI can look for patterns in customers' behavior that may help you understand their wants and needs better. You can apply behavioral psychology to what you see and run an endless series of small tests to see if you're right and to learn more. In a host of ways, the combination of technology and social sciences enables untold new opportunities for companies to make sense of customer behaviors and anticipate their wants.

These developments increase the surface area between the company and the customer—letting you engage more directly and build the right insights from those exchanges.

Developing privileged insights into customers requires much more than just buying market research or buying data from Google—something any competitor can do. (See "The Rise—and Limitations—of Traditional Market Research.") And the effort isn't just a one-time project or the job of a single function. Instead, it's a way of working that seeks insights from across internal functions, ecosystem partners, and customers and assembles the insights into understanding that feeds your value proposition and capabilities system.

In fact, gaining privileged insights may become one of your most important capabilities. It is a prime example of a complex, multifunctional capability that can let you stand out from your competitors as you continually provide products and services that are better tuned to customers' wants and needs and that adapt as those wants and needs evolve. It is a great example of the positive complexity of a capability, as it truly integrates unique digital assets with the tools, processes, and people that bring the capability to life.

Four Steps to Building a System of Privileged Insights

How can you emulate the success of Adobe and other customer insights champions like STC Pay, Philips, IKEA, Komatsu, or Inditex? Here are four steps—roughly sequential—that you can follow.

1. **Establish a foundation of purpose and trust.** Be clear about how you earn customers' trust to engage with you—including impeccable clarity on your values, principles, and governance around how you will treat their data and use your insights.

2. **Lay out a purposeful customer insights approach and road map.** Focus your privileged insights strategy around the key questions that empower your purpose—the questions that would inspire your customers to engage with you. Build your

103

The Rise—and Limitations—of Traditional Market Research

As business organizations evolved through the eighteenth and nineteenth centuries—and even, in some sectors, well into the twentieth century—companies tended to be small enough that "understanding customers" happened organically and extemporaneously. Business owners interacted continually with their customers in the normal course of business. Enormous value was created as a result of this close proximity of the owner to the customer, a proximity that many small businesses have managed to retain. But as companies became larger in the early twentieth century and businesses increasingly focused on realizing scale in production and operations, the connections between companies and their customers often became more distant and diffuse—sales forces, distributors, and wholesalers all came between the CEO and the customer.

About a hundred years ago, the recognition of this growing disconnect gave rise to the market research function. Some of the pioneer management consulting firms, in fact, got their start by conducting research for companies that wanted to "learn about their customers." Edwin G. Booz, for example, one of the earliest US business consultants (and cofounder of one of the corporate antecedents to Strategy&, part of the PwC network), began his career in 1914 by doing customer surveys for railroad companies and other corporations. Soon, companies began analyzing demographic information and sales data to understand customer behavior—and an entire industry sprang up to provide quantitative research for them to use. By mid- to late century, companies were adding new tools and approaches, like focus groups and ethnographic research—which adapted methodologies from cultural anthropology—for observing how consumers behave in everyday situations at home, at work, or in stores. By assessing user experience in a "natural" setting, ethnographic researchers gained insights into the practical applications of a product or service. Those insights enabled what's now called *design thinking* (understanding the user, challenging assumptions, and redefining problems to identify alternative strategies and solutions).

The most common research approach, the quantitative survey instrument, became almost table stakes for organizations to understand their customers. Relying on a basic premise—"Ask questions, create insights, and take action"—many analytical approaches were developed to understand customer choices and buying patterns.

But in the same way that products and services became more commoditized and undifferentiated as companies focused on benchmarking and pursued the realization of benefits of scale, customer research also became more commoditized as companies grew larger. This was the world that brought us mass marketing and mass advertising, of supermarkets and prime-time television commercials—the world of *Mad Men* and the Marlboro Man. It was the world in which General Motors created brands and entire divisions—Chevrolet, Pontiac, Oldsmobile, Buick, and Cadillac—to sell cars targeted to different customer segments.

Today, much of the learning about customers that derives from traditional market research isn't truly differentiated. Anyone who wants to study consumers can launch surveys, convene focus groups, or conduct ethnographic studies—and it sometimes feels like everyone does. The result is an overwhelming proliferation of data, much of it of uncertain quality.

(continued)

Traditional market research can still provide insights, and it will probably be a part of your privileged insights capability, but research can no longer be disconnected from engagement. The rise of digital has given us the ability to observe and analyze much more granular data. We can focus on more specific and detailed customer segments and channels. Rather than asking questions, we can get hints about what consumers may want by looking at what they do or what else they have bought or used.

While you can learn from what people say, you can learn even more from watching what they do.

---

insights capability and road map guided by the problems you seek to solve for your customers.

3. **Build and enhance your mechanisms for gaining customer insights.** Develop new or strengthen existing ways of interacting with your chosen customers and make those mechanisms an integral part of how you operate.

4. **Wire your privileged insights into how you work.** Put your privileged insights to work by connecting them into your operations—including your strategy and innovation capabilities—so you systematically strengthen your value proposition, your capabilities system, and the products and services you offer.

Establish a Foundation of Purpose and Trust

For customers to be willing to share information with you, they must buy into your company's purpose. And they need to be convinced that you're going to make the right use of the data, insights, and confidences they share with you. Purpose and trust are the foundation of your ability to build a privileged insights capability.

The work you did when you determined your place in the world is a foundation for this step. If you've done your work well, the place you've articulated will help customers understand what value you're creating for them and how your purpose is connected to what matters to them. Delivering on your promise is an absolutely critical element of building trust.

In addition, you will need to be crystal clear, on an ethical level, about what you will use customers' information for and how you will use the insights you develop. You will need to articulate and communicate explicit principles and put in place the right governance to enforce them. You also cannot afford any mistakes when it comes to data protection and cybersecurity in the domain of privileged insights. You will need to view your spending in this area not as a cost of doing business to somehow minimize, but as a strategic investment.

Adobe's Ashley Still is absolutely clear about the company's guiding principle for how they use customer data: "We are committed to data privacy and sensitive to how we use data. Responsible use of customer data can create greater experiences, but the second we start using it to gain tactical advantage, we've missed the mark." Leaders must ensure that people across the organization understand that it's not about extracting data from people—it's about making your customers an integral part of the value chain.

Lay Out a Purposeful Customer Insights Approach and Road Map

Building your privileged insights capability inevitably comes with the challenge of defining what insights you should focus on and where to get started. Almost every department in the company could do with more or better insights—whether in the logistics function to understand customer expectations and tolerances around delivery, or in the sales function around the right price-versus-value trade-offs. But with privileged insights, as we define them, we recommend that you anchor your focus around the critical questions and insights that will help you shape your future—the place in the world you are seeking. Yes, you can gain tremendous value by using insights to inform how you can operate better today—and you should do so. At the same time, for companies starting on the privileged insights journey, it is important to have a laser-like focus on answering the key questions that help you tackle the big problems you are aiming to solve for your customers and that will guide your future. Similarly, and as we will discuss later, your value proposition should guide how you engage with your customers so that "collecting insights" is not a separate process.

Don't forget that not every customer may want to enter into an intimate relationship where they willingly share their desires and motivations. You will need to identify a set of customers who represent your best source of privileged insights—those who resonate most with your purpose and to whom you can offer the greatest value. These customers may not necessarily be your company's biggest fans (yet) or even your largest customers. They may not even be customers with whom you have a long relationship or track record.

Take STC Pay, a fintech startup and subsidiary of Saudi Telecom Corporation, as an example. Saudi Telecom set out in 2015 to dramatically change its strategy. One of its new areas of growth was financial services. STC Pay was launched in 2018 to provide innovative technologies and digital experiences to connect individuals and businesses and help them with all their financial services operations. STC Pay started with a "digital wallet" that enables customers to send and receive money, shop, and control finances through a single smartphone app.

"One of the main advantages we had, and we still have, compared to the incumbent players in this market is that we started with a plain white drawing board. Nothing was there," says Saleh Mosaibah, the founding CEO of STC Pay (now Group CEO Advisor of the parent company).

STC Pay's first offering—suggested by the Kingdom of Saudi Arabia's banking regulator, in line with the Kingdom's "Vision 2030" for future growth—was a solution for the country's large population of guest workers. Most typically have no banking relationship and remit the majority of their compensation (85 percent, on average) to family members in their home countries. STC Pay created an easy-to-use mobile-phone app and partnered with Western Union to enable instant payments via 525,000 Western Union locations worldwide.

"Once the remittances business was up and running," says Mosaibah, "we found that, when you master one service, customers come to you with new demands for other services." The company has since added features to attract other Saudi customers in addition to the guest-worker population. These include the ability to pay for purchases by scanning a QR code for an item and for gasoline by authorizing payment at gas stations that have license-plate readers. STC Pay now even offers full payroll services for companies. Says Mosaibah,

> We have customers who are really in love with STC Pay, who passionately give us their feedback and suggestions. They meet us at our events and say, "We're big fans of yours." Their enthusiasm comes from two things. First is the customer experience that we provide—we really alleviate a number of their pain points. Second is them seeing us being really responsive. Usually when you send feedback on social media or in other ways, you don't expect quick responses. With STC Pay, you do. We pick up a lot of ideas from these fans, and we implement them. We're working on further discovering and cultivating these people.

One example of how this feedback turns into new services: STC Pay's "shared accounts." Wealthy Saudi customers, Mosaibah explains, "typically have large families and staffs of domestic workers." STC Pay customers wanted to be able to give money to relatives or domestic workers but keep some control over what the recipients did with the money. The company therefore designed a new concept. Mosaibah says, "You can create a shared account, define the recurring monthly limit, determine who gets the money, and [limit] what they can do with that money." Domestic workers, for example, can be authorized to make payments at gas stations or grocery stores. Family members might be authorized to pay at restaurants or specified shops or websites, or to withdraw cash from ATMs. The account owner can see all the transactions in real time and, at any point, change the permissions or close the shared account.

All of STC Pay's designs start from personas, which allow the company to put itself into the shoes of its customers, experiencing what these people are struggling with, what they need, and how it can address those needs. For example, one persona is Mohammed, a merchant whose employer doesn't trust him and always asks for invoices when he pays for something. It's STC Pay's unique, privileged insights that allow it to create these customer models and make sure that its offerings are truly valuable.

"The financial industry is being disrupted because fintech companies like us went to the basic, core principles of banking, which is helping people manage their money," says Mosaibah. "Banks forgot about this principle. We came along and said, 'What do you need, dear customer?' We don't really care if people think we're reinventing banking or not. We care about whether we really help people. Do we really add value to them?"

STC Pay's approach rooted in privileged insights into customers has paid off: Only two years after launch, STC Pay achieved a billion-dollar valuation, which made it the first unicorn in the Kingdom and the first fintech unicorn in the Middle East. It is now gearing up to expand its services into the UAE, Kuwait, and Bahrain.[3]

As STC Pay shows, even a company without a long history can develop a privileged relationship with customers if they feel valued and see their needs being met uniquely. Customers will want to be part of improving that product, service, or experience and will be more likely to share information that will give you unique and valuable insights.

Build and Enhance Your Mechanisms for Gaining Customer Insights

Every company gets customer feedback, but not every company builds a privileged insights capability. When you start to think about building or enhancing that capability, you will probably recognize that you have more access to information about your customers than you may have thought and than you're currently leveraging. Using that existing information can already improve your understanding of your customers—but don't stop there.

Ask yourself how you can strengthen your current ways of interacting with customers to get more insights, or what new ways of interacting you can put in place. How can you make sure these mechanisms are fully integrated with how you operate—not a thing you do on the side, sporadically, that will run out of steam? Your interactions for gaining customer insights should ideally be part of what you anyhow do to deliver your value proposition to your customers, bringing insights and customer experience together. The many direct-to-consumer businesses that have erupted in many consumer-facing industries are a good example of this.

A variety of methods can work. Some companies bet on personal observation of what customers do and how they use products—or could use products if only they existed. Others look for technology-enabled solutions. Others go as far as changing their entire business model to get close to their customers. Whichever path you choose, a deeply human connection is needed. If you don't really listen to customers and care about helping them overcome pain points, you're not going to succeed.

Philips, for example, uses the exceptional access it has to hospitals and other medical facilities to gain insights about what customers need now—and anticipate what they may want in the future. Carla Kriwet, former chief business leader of Philips's Connected Care and Health Informatics division (and member of Philips's executive committee), for example, spent a week each year doing a traineeship at a hospital, following doctors or nurses on their rounds. "I do it to understand how they're using our devices, what their concerns are and, frankly, just find out what's on their minds and how they feel," she says. Several years ago, Kriwet was accompanying a young nurse, just out of university, on her rounds. She recalls that the nurse was passionate about her work but completely overwhelmed by being responsible for twelve patients in one of the hospital's general wards. "We went to the first patient, and he was not in great condition. The nurse did a series of checks, but nothing was obviously wrong," Kriwet says. The nurse and Kriwet left this patient to attend to requests from two others. As they returned and walked past the first patient's bed, Kriwet recalls, "The nurse found that his condition was deteriorating, and then the patient suddenly died." The patient had had a heart attack, but there had been no way to predict it; since he was in the general ward rather than the ICU, he was not connected to the kind of sophisticated monitor that might have sensed the developing problem. These machines are large, expensive, and not mobile, and thus are not suitable for use in the general wards.

Kriwet had her team develop a simplified, wearable, mobile bio-sensor that connects to the hospital's patient monitoring system. "It takes basic vital signs—respiratory rate, heart rate, and temperature," says Kriwet. "It uses smart algorithms to help clinicians detect risk so they can intervene. It can have a real impact."

IKEA is another example of a company that continually refines its means of understanding customers by improving its access to people—placing itself in the same frame of mind as its customers and developing a better feel for their wishes, frustrations, and attitudes. One of its main methods has been "home visits"—house calls made by its managers and staff to better understand how people live. (Each year, IKEA co-workers do hundreds of home visits around the world.)

The company has extended this approach by identifying customers in Stockholm, Milan, New York, and Shenzhen who are willing to have video cameras put in their homes. The insights IKEA gains about how people live, and what their frustrations, needs, and dreams are, enable the company to create innovative products. In recent years, these insights have helped IKEA develop more sensitivity to the needs of young adults and single adults of all ages. People who grow older without children tend to live in small urban apartments, and their social lives and homes are quite different from those of the families and students who constituted IKEA's original core market. One example: after observing the irritations customers experience getting ready for work each morning, IKEA devised the Knapper—a freestanding mirror with a rack for clothes and jewelry that makes it easy for customers to put together an outfit the night before work and get out the door more quickly in the morning. If you find yourself surprised at the level of access IKEA has gained, think about how much trust these consumers must have to partake in the process.

Some companies even change their business model to gain privileged insights into customers. For example, some companies move from selling stand-alone products and services to selling solutions or experiences. The change allows them to significantly deepen their relationships with customers and gain insights they could not have imagined.

Until recently, for example, Komatsu had seen itself primarily as making and selling construction equipment and had spent fifty years perfecting its products via TQM and QC. "We were always looking at things from a manufacturer's perspective," recalls Tetsuji Ohashi, chairman of the board and former CEO. "We made products, sold them to customers, and made sure that customers were satisfied. The only topics that would come up in our discussions with customers were that [they hoped] the machinery wouldn't break down, or that it needed to be repaired right away if it did break down."

As we discussed in chapter 3, starting in 2013, Komatsu began to focus on incorporating information and communication technology (ICT) into machinery as part of a move toward "smart construction," which aims to significantly improve the efficiency and effectiveness of construction sites. That efficiency is a key goal in Japan, where changing demographics have led to a persistent shortage of construction workers. But given how new the technology was, Komatsu needed much better understanding of their customers to be able to focus its efforts.

Leadership therefore decided to change the business model and rent equipment rather than sell new machines. Chikashi Shike, executive officer and president of the Smart Construction Promotion Division, recalls: "Had we continued to sell the machinery, we would not have had a way of knowing what changes would occur on construction sites as a result of ICT machinery being used. But we wanted to be able to identify any problems that came up early on and find out why site productivity may not improve as expected when ICT machinery was being used."

This change in business model allowed Komatsu to have much more touchpoints with the actual users of the machinery (as opposed to the procurement department) and get information from their customers about how the products were being used and the kinds of worksite issues customers faced. "This was an important step in building lasting, long-term relationships with customers by making ourselves essential to their businesses, rather than simply engaging in transactions where we sell a product, and that's it on relationship," Shike explains.

The insights Komatsu gained were eye-opening. Adding ICT to machines increased worksite productivity much less than expected.

The technology worked well—but couldn't resolve bottlenecks that occurred in the processes prior to and after the actual construction work; for example, with the surveying or with hauling dirt away. This recognition led Komatsu to create a Smart Construction Promotion Division and move beyond selling, renting, and servicing machinery. The mandate became much bigger: to create solutions that would enable customers to understand and shape future construction sites to improve productivity. This new approach required the company to develop Landlog, its open platform (see chapter 3), to bring together data from people, machinery, materials, and geography across the construction process to better coordinate and manage construction programs— shifting Komatsu's role from being just another provider of machinery to occupying a central role in the construction industry.

Whatever approach you take, use this opportunity not just to build a new "customer data" capability but to reimagine how you interact with your customers.

Wire Your Privileged Insights into How You Work

Gaining privileged insights alone does not generate a whole lot of value. You need to connect these insights with your strategy and innovation capabilities and ultimately into your day-to-day operations, so you can refine your value proposition and improve your ability to deliver on it. How is customers' perception of value changing? What is it that they want now, and will want in the future? How do they perceive the outcome your capabilities generate? What would you need to do to wow them? Answers to these questions will help you evolve your value proposition, make improvements to your capabilities so they deliver more relevant value for your customers, and offer products, services, solutions and experiences that are going to keep your customers coming back to you, time and time again. When you wire your privileged insights into how you work in this way, your privileged insights start working for you—helping you live up to your promise to customers, stay in front of their needs, and continually enhance the value you create.

Privileged insights have to be a strategic initiative. In addition to having someone at the executive level owning the insights agenda and how you put it to work, every executive needs to have account-ability and demonstrate how they're putting the insights to work. Consider Inditex's Zara. Its rise in fast fashion shows a company where customer insights are its lifeblood. Jesús Echevarría, chief communication officer, explains: "You need to be honest to really give customers what they are asking for. This may seem very simple. But it actually is really difficult, because human beings are always trying to do what they want. Designers are inclined to develop what they like best. Distributors want to ship what makes most sense for them. Store assistants tend to display things in their own way. It takes real discipline to put everyone's assumptions, beliefs, and preferences to the side and really listen to what the customer is asking."

Inditex's culture is of great help to get everyone focused on under-standing customers. "This company has been created with a culture of understanding and giving people what they are going to like," Eche-varría continues, "We feel satisfied when customers are satisfied—there's nothing better than that for us. Our designers may think that one of their designs is the best thing they ever realized. But if customers don't like it, designers will forget about the design and not push it."

Understanding what customers like is critical to Inditex's success. Its business model is based on adapting production to demand, which allows for minimizing dead stock. The company's retail employees are trained to serve as the company's frontline eyes and ears, tracking data, observing customers, and gathering informal impressions. The stores compile information about the choices customers make, their inquiries about missing items, and their suggestions. Are shoppers looking for skirts or trousers? Bold or subtle colors? These impressions are sent directly to a group of designers and operational experts at headquarters, who are charged with translating them immediately into new products for the racks.[4] The key is in the flexibility to adapt to customer preferences and the precision to create and produce what customers are asking for, at the moment they are asking for it.

The company is embracing digital technology in its characteristic way: farsighted and pragmatic. Inditex is incorporating only those innovations that fit its strategic goals. It isn't experimenting, for example, with garments made to order. But it is integrating its online and offline retail stores, doubling down on the sustainability and quality of materials, and using its distinctive tracking system to become even more responsive and successful in monitoring.

One technological change is particularly noteworthy. As described in chapter 1, thanks to RFID chips it puts in each of its garments— something virtually unheard of when Inditex began its digital transformation back in 2013—the company can now know, in real time, how many units of every item sell anywhere around the globe and also have individual tracking of garments, from the logistics platforms until their ultimate sale. But Inditex doesn't just aggregate and analyze the data. It sets up an intense process of making sense of the data and getting insights out of it. The process has three layers: the stores themselves, where managers know how local holidays, the weather, or the particular store displays may have impacted sales; regional teams that compare what's happening across stores; and managers at headquarters. Those managers are specialized in men's, women's, or children's wear. They analyze all the information to understand what's happening on a daily basis and see what customers are liking.

Echevarría says, "All this information is shared with designers who are going to react to what customers are doing. They're creating new waves of collections based on the information that comes from the stores as well as the analysis performed by regional and headquarters teams. Given all those insights, they are able to say, 'Okay, here we know that in our region, the red jacket that you have created has been very well-received, so we bet that this is a good choice now.'" Designers create a file that is translated into a sample and discussed with country managers, designers, the purchasing team, and the retail team. It's this cross-functional collaboration that allows Inditex to be so flexible: at the end of the year, Inditex's more than seven hundred designers will have come up with sixty thousand different creations, and the stores worldwide will have received new waves of collections twice per week.

Inditex's success is for the most part due to this system of insights. The company knows what people are asking for and saying in its stores and—in real time—exactly what is selling and where. These insights are rolled up, aggregated, scaled, and analyzed almost in real time and turned into designs for new garments or into improved production, logistics, and marketing practices. The flexibility of its business model, coupled with an integrated stock management, gives Inditex the ability to react swiftly to unfolding market circumstances and work with reduced stock levels.

If you're collecting data on customers and it's piling up, that's a clear sign that you haven't yet figured out how to harness the power of privileged insights. But when gaining information becomes part of the process of how you do business and how you deliver value, then you've built a capability that will power you forward. And not just for today: you'll have a well-engineered, scalable system for continuously evolving your value proposition and making it more relevant, and for reinforcing and renewing your capabilities based on insights that your competitors lack.

. . .

So far, we have focused on how companies need to transform in relation to their markets, their ecosystems, and their customers—all largely outside the company itself. In the next four chapters, we will look deeply inside the company—at the organization, the leadership team, the social contract with the workforce, and the personal transformation that leaders themselves need.

5

Make Your Organization Outcome-Oriented

The five separate fingers are five independent units. Close them and the fist multiplies strength. This is organization.

—James Cash Penney, founder of JC Penney stores

In the late 1990s, leaders at Honeywell's Aerospace division began to think about how advances in digitization, communications, and connectivity might create opportunities in its aviation businesses. Those businesses made products like engines, brakes, navigation gear, and avionics. They also provided services like airplane maintenance and flight information software.

"We had a lot of ideas about what we could do with connectivity and what it could mean for our businesses back then," recalls Carl Esposito, formerly president of Honeywell's Electronic Solutions business unit (responsible for cockpit systems, navigation, space, and safety systems businesses). But, he adds, "We needed the technology to catch up [to the company's vision]." Cell phones were not yet connected to the Web; geo-positioning and communications satellites were still largely optimized for military rather than commercial usage; the term "Internet of Things" had been introduced, but initially just to promote RFID technology; and cloud computing was in its infancy.

Ten years later, however, technologies were catching up fast. Smartphones had gone online and become part of everyday life. Military restrictions on satellite usage had been relaxed, and more commercial satellites were orbiting the earth. The Internet of Things had begun to take on its present role as the information backbone of industry and commerce. Cloud computing had come of age. By 2010, Honeywell Aerospace was mapping out the ways the division's products and services could be brought together as a "connected aircraft" business that would add significantly more customer value than the sum of its parts, for example by offering real-time solutions for aviation customers, such as improved power and fuel usage, predictive maintenance, more precise flight planning, and real-time, crowdsourced weather information.

To fully benefit from the opportunity, Honeywell had to add capabilities in connectivity and communications to the aerospace division's existing strengths in manufacturing and services. It did this via acquisition and partnerships. In 2011, Honeywell acquired EMS Technologies, which specialized in airborne communications devices and systems. The next year, Honeywell entered an exclusive partnership with Inmarsat, the global satellite services provider, to provide in-flight connectivity services to aviation customers around the world.

Adding those communications and connectivity capabilities wasn't enough. They had to be integrated fully into Honeywell's everyday way of working. Once corporate leadership green-lighted the new connected aircraft business, Honeywell realized that a major reorganization of its aviation product and services business would be needed to bring the right people, skills, and capabilities together. "In aviation," says Esposito, "we've built planes forever in a very methodical, structured way, where we have functions that are really separate and segregated. We built them piece by piece, as opposed to thinking holistically. It was difficult to cross boundaries between engines and avionics and electronics—but that's exactly what was needed now because connectivity was really transformational across all those products."

In early 2014, Mike Edmonds, then divisional SVP in charge of services and connectivity—a small business at the time—was to present a business review at an executive committee meeting. He was proud because he had managed to expand the margins of the business significantly. While celebrating this success, the executive committee asked him what it would take to grow the top line of the business commensurate with what he had done on the bottom line. Edmonds said he would come back with a plan in thirty days. "Come back in three hours," the committee told him. "We think you know what to do."

Edmonds, indeed, did have the outlines of a plan—but he had not vetted it with anyone, a dangerous move in the Honeywell culture. In what he recalls as a light bulb moment, when the meeting reconvened, he asked the executive committee for radical organizational changes: bringing IT, data analytics, and engineering people from their home functions into one team and granting authority to hire new product managers and team members with data analytics skills. Tim Mahoney, then CEO of Honeywell Aerospace, said: "Okay. I want the new positions to be posted by the end of the day. And I want these IT, data analysis, and engineering people to report to Mike [Edmonds] and be moved over by the end of the week."

As the transformation got underway, new teams were tasked with rethinking how legacy offerings that had existed as stand-alone products could be reimagined to operate in a broader, networked environment. Leaders needed to identify specific types of persons to make it all work. "What we needed," Esposito recalls, "was people that could step out of their technical expertise in their functional area and think about the larger problems we were trying to solve." He refers to these people as "translators," who were able to facilitate discussion between, for example, different technical specialists such as wheels and brakes, avionics, and connectivity and were also able to communicate with marketing and product management specialists. "Once people began to understand the different way these teams talked, the floodgates of ideas opened, and people started to really see the vision and where this could go."

By 2015–2016, Honeywell was starting to roll out some of its most promising ideas, including GoDirect Connected Maintenance. The solution analyzes aircraft data and delivers diagnostics as well as predictive, prescriptive alerts; it allows for up to 35 percent savings on maintenance. GoDirect also provides connected weather radar that shares data between planes, much as Waze crowdsources traffic information for motorists. In addition, GoDirect offers high-speed WiFi access for flight crews and passengers.

In 2019, the company introduced Honeywell Forge, a next-level connectivity solution that uses advanced data analytics to deliver a comprehensive portfolio of in-flight connectivity, flight planning and optimization, and flight database services.

New ways of thinking were needed not just in product development but across the entire organization. "We spent a huge amount of time developing training programs and doing internal communication to help our employees be able to tell the simple story," says Kristin Slyker, former vice president of Connected Aircraft. "We've been helping them communicate analogies for connected aircrafts; for example, talking about the fact that a connected aircraft is a little bit like a cellular phone. We sell hardware—for example, an antenna—that is like the phone itself. We partner with Inmarsat to bring airtime services—that is, like Verizon or Orange. And, finally, we develop apps or software applications, like flight efficiency applications, that help customers save fuel."

A lot of change was needed in the sales organization, traditionally used to selling expensive components like engines rather than selling services or solutions. "It was more appealing for a salesperson to sell a quarter-million-dollar avionics upgrade than to sell a ten-year maintenance plan for $25,000 per year," says Edmonds, "even though the total dollars might be the same."

But Honeywell stayed the course, constantly reaffirming the importance of the transformation. In addition to structural changes, leadership also changed salespeople's incentive structures, requiring them to sell a minimum amount of services to make their numbers. The company also provided in-depth training, so salespeople felt more comfortable "talking connected." Says Edmonds,

> We realized we had to grow our focus well beyond our own product set and address customer problems. My best customer meetings are when I go in with no slides at all and I sit down and introduce myself and then say, "I'm really interested in your problems. Could you tell me what your biggest delay and cancellation drivers are?" and get them talking about what's on their mind. If they give me some of their data to look into a specific maintenance problem, I can look for other maintenance issues or even flight services problems for the pilot, as well, and then go back in with a solution. That's a very different way of selling from what we used to do.

Honeywell's connected journey isn't done yet, but it's making great progress transforming from an industrial company to the software enabled industrial of the future. Today, Honeywell Connected Aircraft is an $800 million business and is considered by many analysts to be the market leader in the connected aircraft space. The Honeywell Forge flight efficiency platform marks another important step in setting the way: the system was adopted by 128 airlines and more than ten thousand aircraft globally in its first year on the market.

Honeywell's Connected Aircraft story illustrates many of the leadership imperatives we have mentioned before. The company looked ahead at what its customers' real challenges were, redefined its place around a much bolder value proposition, integrated the right technology, and then moved customers in that direction. It leveraged advances in technology not to copy what others were doing but to build its own differentiated value proposition. It pursued acquisitions to build differentiating capabilities. It worked more closely with its ecosystem. But then Honeywell also changed the fundamental way it was organized to work. It invested in enabling mechanisms like training and development and incentive structures to help people break out of the old model and work in the new way. And, all along this journey, the leadership team stepped up and acted decisively.

. . .

Many companies today face the same kinds of challenges that Honeywell faced. The way you will create value is changing. You will need to build, enhance, and integrate your key capabilities into a powerful value-creation engine to help you differentiate in your new place in the world. Building that engine and constantly pushing the limits of what's possible is a Herculean task, and you will need to focus all your organizational energy on delivering the outcomes those capabilities require.

With the model of value creation changing and your success depending on scaling up these complex capabilities, how you work must change, and your organization must be redesigned to support that new way of working. Like Honeywell, you will need to bring broad and diverse roles, skills, and talents together to deliver value that your competitors can't match. You will need people to collaborate fluidly, focused on the outcomes of their work. It's also highly likely that you will need to collaborate with partners and people outside the boundaries of your traditional organization. And because you will need to continuously innovate, strengthen, and adapt your capabilities to respond quickly to market needs, you will need an organization that can, in many ways, be self-directed.

Most organizations are not set up for this kind of flexible, collaborative, and outcome-oriented work. They continue to operate within more rigid organizational constructs that were designed for the work of previous centuries.

The Capabilities-Based Organization: Re-architect Your Traditional Structure

Winning in the beyond digital world requires a new model of organization and teaming. Jeroen Tas, Philips's former chief innovation and strategy officer, makes it clear: "You need diverse teams to solve real challenges. You may want to develop the next iteration of your proposition. That can't be done by R&D engineers only. You may have a big account that you want to win. You don't do it just with salespeople. You may have a supply chain problem. You're not going to solve it with just logistic experts. We've had a hundred years of functional decomposition. We now need to bring it back to craftsmanship; we need to tie different things together. And we have to recognize that we need different types of teams for different purposes."

This new model isn't about plucking people out of their functional roles and asking them to work together 10 or 20 percent of their time, or for six weeks or six months (which is how most companies use cross-functional teams; see "Transcending the Traditional Functional Model"). It's about building more durable, *outcome-oriented teams* tasked with generating the outcome that each of your differentiating capabilities requires for you to be able to deliver on your value proposition. And since your company's differentiating capabilities aren't mono-functional, these teams must bring together everything they need from across the organization and your ecosystem.

Transcending the Traditional Functional Model

Most companies' organizational models can trace their roots back to the nineteenth century. Some of the first business functionaries were railroad telegraph operators who managed schedules. Then came sales forces, finance departments, and R&D labs—including the original labs of Thomas Edison and Alexander Graham Bell. As companies grew larger and more diverse, they started adding business unit and regional organizational structures to better serve individual markets, ultimately creating matrixed organizations where most people had two reporting lines—a functional one and a business unit/region-specific one. In most cases, HR people would continue to work largely on HR-related work only, and finance people would work largely on finance only, leading to what's often perceived as functional silos.

Functions have always played a key role in the development of functional expertise, the upskilling of employees, and the provision of functional career paths. This role, however, has come under fire in the beyond digital age because of the sheer explosion of skills and specificity of capabilities that are required for companies to compete, let alone win. Just think about what it means to be good at marketing these days: analytics, user experience design, buyer behavior understanding, digital asset management, social media engagement, public relations, branding, advertising, and many more skills are needed. There isn't a generic marketeer anymore, nor is there a generic marketing career path or a generic marketing upskilling effort. The skills needed have become much more intricate and specialized.

This has led to companies assessing which skills they should own and which skills they're better off accessing from their ecosystem. While companies have gotten used to relying on outside talent in specific areas like public relations or creative development where they lack the opportunities to attract, develop, and retain great talent, they now need to adopt that way of thinking across a much wider range of skills—focusing on the areas in which they have sufficient scale and an ability to attract top talent, and tapping into a greatly expanded ecosystem to provide unique skills everywhere else.

Despite these developments, the fundamental challenge is that the traditional model, where leaders focus on "functional excellence" and build large functional organizations almost by default results in their losing sight of the end outcome that needs to be achieved. Motivations and incentives can get skewed: while Operations may strive for standard runs, R&D wants exquisite customization; while Sales wants to satisfy customers, Service aims at managing costs. Another challenge is that functions tend to measure themselves against industry functional benchmarks rather than doing unconventional things that help further the company's very specific strategy. It is extremely difficult for functions on their own to build the future when the company's most impactful work is inherently cross-functional.

The path to building and scaling differentiating capabilities in today's value-creation model, however, requires more cross-functional expertise and collaboration. It's not enough to rely on the finance person doing a great job on finance work and then handing off to the next function. Today, the finance person also has to, for example, learn data analytics skills, know how to work with technology, and work symbiotically with the sales, marketing, and operations functions to help accurately forecast and match supply

(continued)

with demand and price products and services at exactly the right levels. The finance person has to be just as aligned and motivated to deliver the operational efficiency, revenue, and profit goals as the operations production supervisor, sales manager, or the marketing product manager. They all have to become much more outcome-oriented versus functional output–oriented. This is especially true as the differentiating capabilities needed for success become more complex and cross-functional, requiring the rapid stitching together and continuous improvement of insights, skills, processes, data, and technology from across the company.

The human technology that has been created to address these challenges—"cross-functional teams"—that bring together different functions and units to achieve a specific objective or project, is becoming ubiquitous in many organizations. Consider, for example, cross-functional engineering teams with members from customer service, manufacturing, R&D, and product marketing groups that come together to solve a quality problem. These teams can work well for targeted efforts like projects, initiatives, change programs, and communications initiatives. But they have proven unsuccessful in generating sustained value creation. That's because in many cases they lack the staying power and influence to really make a difference, and their members have many functional responsibilities that take priority over what the team is supposed to achieve. If functions continue to own talent and influence the direction of careers, they will always win in the race to define agendas and focus—no matter how well intentioned the cross-functional team. Often these teams don't get the best talent; they lack clear targets, metrics, and incentives tied to the desired outcome; and they don't have the clout at senior decision-making levels that the importance of the task would necessitate. These teams are occasionally a useful tool, but they are not the blueprint for building a house.

Other companies have attempted to solve this challenge by overlaying end-to-end process models and roles on top of the traditional matrix organization. In other words, they maintain the traditional functional and business unit matrix, but tell people how to hand off work from one step to another to make collaboration more efficient. While these end-to-end process models may be necessary when you're implementing new enterprise resource planning systems that cut across functions, they typically aren't the solution to your challenges for how to create value. Indeed, they usually end up as a complicated exercise of mapping "standard" process flows and adding another decision-making checkpoint (in the form of global process owners) to the organization to manage and validate that people follow the process. But what do you do when you have to react rapidly in today's world and go outside the blueprinted process to do what is necessary to win in the market? End-to-end process models are invariably rigid and of limited help when the traditional functional matrix model remains the superstructure of the organization.

No matter how great a process is, it's hard to replicate the agility and ingenuity of people working together as one team with a common aim.

For these outcome-oriented teams to succeed, they will need to:

- Be long-lived. Since the capabilities they create are at the heart of the company's success, these teams need to be here to stay. Their size and composition, however, can change over time as the capabilities themselves evolve.

- Have team members who are dedicated full-time to building and scaling the differentiating capabilities you have chosen; the capabilities are too important to be a "task on the side."

- Have their own resources—people and budgets—rather than borrowing from functions and business units. If differentiating capabilities are key to your company's success, that needs to be reflected in how you allocate budgets and investments.

- Be led by senior executives, typically members of the company's top team, who have an equal seat at the decision-making table of the company.

We've seen a number of companies change their organizational structures and create select outcome-oriented teams that are long-lived and cross-boundary. These have become common in the innovation capability in particular, where companies have broken down traditional silos between R&D and other functions such as customer insight, marketing, sales, service, operations, and finance. These teams focus on innovation as a truly integrated capability, working across the whole organization. Their members are not "on loan" to the innovation teams, they are part of a fully operational outcome-oriented team, and work together as a clear unit. Many include ecosystem partners and customers outside the traditional organizational boundaries in the team. Similarly, hospitals have created patient experience teams that focus on improving patient outcomes and satisfaction and that coordinate departments such as cardiology, intensive care, nursing, and physical therapy.

Other examples include: total quality teams (integrating people from across R&D, manufacturing, supply chain, logistics, marketing, sales, finance, and customer service), customer experience teams (combining people from across the value chain to own and shape the customer journey), and revenue growth management and in-market execution teams in consumer product goods companies (integrating finance, marketing, sales, data, technology, and supply chain).

In the new, capabilities-based organization, outcome-oriented teams sit alongside functions and focus on delivering the company's differentiated capabilities. These teams coexist with the corporate center, business units, and functions/shared services (see figure 5-1), but increasingly become more prominent elements of the organization. In many organizations, we see that the majority of functional headcount gets embedded within outcome-oriented teams and rotates across different teams and business units to develop broader skills and collaborative ways of working. In fact, the bulk of organizational budgets and headcount spending shifts from traditional functional leaders toward outcome-oriented teams, enabling those teams to drive the company's priorities around differentiating capabilities in a coherent way. In short, the implementation of outcome-oriented teams aligns the organization's structure with the most important work that needs to be done to deliver the outcomes that matter to your value proposition and to your customers.

Thus, in the capabilities-based organization, purely functional teams become more focused on specialized mono-functional work (for example, investor relations or labor relations) and driving functional expertise (for example, by shaping policies and procedures, establishing the appropriate governance over functional expertise, sharing and growing functional best practices across the organization, and developing the functional talent and skills needed to feed the rest of the organization). While still critical to the company's success, in this model, functions directly manage a smaller universe, but indirectly influence and support the value creation model across the organization. Their role remains important, but with more indirect influence and guidance versus direct ownership of the majority of activities.

Some readers may recognize a form of this model in the expanding scope and role of their shared services organizations over the last two decades. The old shared services model of transaction centers that consolidate transactional functional activities (for example, accounts payable and accounts receivable) has today evolved in many organizations toward more integrated global providers of cross-functionally integrated end-to-end business outcome services (for example, working capital optimization) enabled by digital and data

FIGURE 5-1

From the traditional organization to the capabilities-based organization

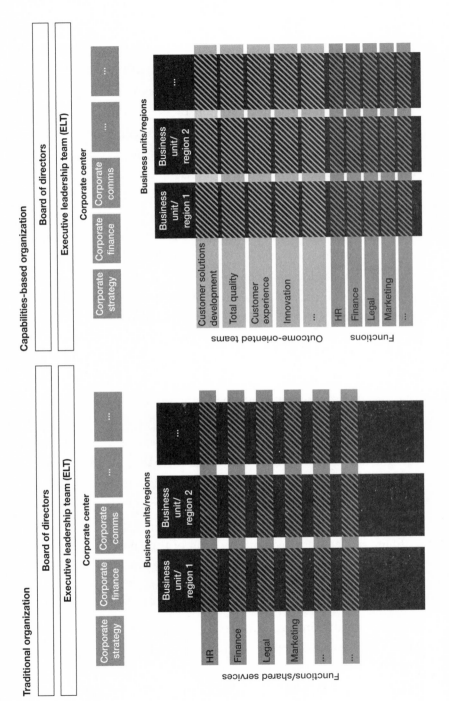

Source: Strategy&.

insights capabilities. In many organizations, these outcome-oriented business services groups have become the largest owners of headcount—including both company employees and external partners. We see this phenomenon as one leading indicator of the capabilities-based organization that will become more prominent as more companies go beyond digital.

Business units, in this new model, become even more customer- and market-centric (and less product-centric) and play an increasingly important integration role to ensure capabilities are appropriately shaped toward customer needs. This integration role is very distinct from the old "general management" role, being focused more on how to interface with the customer versus organizing all of the activities needed to deliver. The business unit role, indeed, becomes much more about assembling the output of outcome-oriented teams in ways that meet customer-specific requirements.

Creating the right set of outcome-oriented teams starts with clearly defining your differentiating capabilities and the outcomes they need to generate—not what they are able to generate today, but what they *need* to generate for your company to deliver your re-imagined place in the world. This capability blueprint defines what expertise, knowledge, technology, data, processes, and behaviors are required in what way to deliver the desired outcome—just like the architectural blueprint defines how every aspect of a structure must come together. The capability blueprint will help you identify people with the right skills you need to put together and empower to work across the old boundaries to deliver the outcomes you need. Where to start? The more important the capability for your company's value creation and the more diverse the skills that are needed, the more urgent the need to act.

In many companies, the transition from the functional to the outcome-oriented organization model does not happen overnight, with a big bang. But given the urgency for companies to build the capabilities required to deliver their reimagined place, they will need to think about how to accelerate the transition. Carefully assess how to phase changes so you bring the most important capabilities online, and the right resources together.

In some organizations, companies start adopting new ways of working such as agile methodologies—bringing together people from across functions with nonhierarchical roles to work in structured sprints to support problem solving of complex topics. And in other organizations, shared service centers or even entirely new teams are asked to take on new capability development. While these may be helpful steps, they are often not sufficient in themselves to achieve the kind of transformation required in the organization's way of working. In fact, if not part of a larger change, sometimes these new teams will struggle to have impact, being seen as "pirate ships" without the ability to integrate in the overall organization.

Microsoft's Journey to a Capabilities-Based Organization

Microsoft began a transformation after the appointment of Satya Nadella as CEO in 2014, in a "renewal of Microsoft." The case for change was obvious: quarterly shipments of PCs had slumped to 70 million, while smartphone shipments were rocketing past 350 million. This was bad news for Microsoft, since 75 percent of its revenue came from Windows software preinstalled on PCs. To make things worse, the company had made little headway in mobile or other rising technologies like cloud computing, social media, software-as-a-service solutions, and big data. It was hard to see how Microsoft would succeed in the rapidly evolving technology market.

Jean-Philippe Courtois, executive vice president and president of Microsoft Global Sales, Marketing and Operations, remembers, "It was very clear to us that what got us there twenty-five years ago would not get us here in the future. The mission we had as a company, that one day there would be 'a computer on every desk, in every home,' had been fantastic; it had really carried us forward. But it was insufficient. So we developed a new worldview: 'With the magnitude of change going on around us, every company in the world is going to become a digital company, and every person in the world needs to become digitally native. And the world is becoming a cloud-first, obviously mobile-first, world.'"

How could they help their customers digitally transform if they had fallen so behind? On his first day as CEO, Nadella announced a new strategy of "mobile first, cloud first," which later evolved to "AI/ cloud first." Microsoft's old mission statement—"a computer on every desk, in every home"—was retired and replaced with "To empower every person and every organization on the planet to achieve more." The former was about selling products to customers; the latter is about providing outcomes—in other words, solutions—for customers.

"The transformation we had to undertake was huge," says Courtois:

> We started this journey with the legacy people, skills, organizations, processes, tools, and capabilities of a company that was used to license software agreements to customers, the smallest and largest in the world, with little ongoing customer interaction afterwards. And now we understood that our new worldview required us to shift away from being a software-oriented company to being a cloud-oriented one. That meant, for example, that we had to completely change the pace of innovation, away from what used to be three- to four-year software release cycles to teams that are creating new services and solutions every few weeks.

And it also meant that Microsoft would have to focus much more on driving consumption of cloud services by its customers.

One of the key organizational changes underpinning Microsoft's refresh was the transformation of the company's global commercial business. The change was a massive undertaking. Over several months, seventy executives and some four hundred senior managers developed a strategy, unveiled in February 2017, that profoundly changed the way Microsoft's commercial division goes to market. The transformation was organized around five pillars to bring the right resources to the right customer at the right time, enabling Microsoft to support its customers with their digital transformation and drive consumption:

- **Industry coverage.** The company restructured the sales organization around specific industries to provide tailored expertise and services to help customers transform; the former approach had involved acting more as a software or infrastructure-service provider.

- **Technical expertise.** It brought technical competency closer to the customers by including engineers in field sales teams.

- **Customer success.** It promoted usage and consumption of cloud services by more deeply engaging with customers both pre- and post-sale; often, Microsoft engineers, consultants, and developers worked on-site.

- **Digital selling.** It empowered the sales force by using digital infrastructure and AI.

- **One commercial partner.** The company simplified the rules of engagement between ecosystem partners and its own sales organization to enable partners to serve customers more effectively.

Some of the key organizational changes were designed to move the company away from its traditional functions—presales, sales, and post-sales—to more specialized roles better aligned with customers' needs. These included realigning specialized account-team units to better support the company's enterprise accounts (the top accounts) with industry experts. The changes also involved refocusing specialist team units—comprising solution specialists and technical solution professionals—to focus on acquiring new customers and delivering technical support to existing customers. In addition, the changes meant creating a customer success unit to demonstrate the value of the cloud to enterprise customers, induce the adoption of more services, and increase consumption. With all these diverse skills coming together, Microsoft's new outcome-oriented teams were well positioned to deliver on the company's new place in the world. "We also have an overlay of what we call the 'global black belt team' who work on top, at the global or regional level, to help on even more advanced capabilities," says Courtois.

There were two key reasons why Microsoft organized this way. As Courtois explains, "The first reason is because we need that multifaceted set of skills and ways of working in order to accompany our customers along the cycle of their transformation. Every company is becoming a software company. That's much more than just moving a bunch of virtual machines to the cloud—it's about building new businesses and new models. We need all those capabilities to become much more intimate with our customers' businesses and their business strategies."

The second reason is cultural. Microsoft had been a product-centric company, and if it wanted to become a "customer-obsessed company" (as it calls itself) it had to organize differently. Courtois argues,

> We've got to support our customers' transformation, from beginning to end: First, we need to envision the digital capabilities our customers need. Then we've got to work with our customers on what is the right technology architecture to build that capability, based on their legacy architecture and who they are as a company. And then we need to translate

that into many projects at a much faster pace in order to create digital products, digital operations, digital customer journeys, etc. In order to drive this culture change, we had to create a very different kind of organization capability on the ground.

When the new organization went live on July 1, 2017, the jobs of forty thousand people in Global Sales, Marketing and Operations, as well as the Worldwide Commercial Business, changed overnight—from the most common role or account executive on up.

"We changed the roles of 90 percent of our leaders and about 80 percent of non-leaders. It was a fairly major change," recalls Nicola Hodson, vice president of Field Transformation in Global Sales, Marketing and Operations:

> We had about six months before launching on July 1, 2017, in order to plan, test, and start to bring layers of leadership onboard with the changes. We put a lot of effort and planning into building a coalition of support. We started with a small core team, doing the planning work and the design. We expanded that to take on more field people to test it properly. Then, we took genuine time and space to bring on area leaders and their leadership teams. By the end of May, we had spoken to all of our leaders. We had explained the changes to them. We had appointed them into the new roles, and they were all secure and ready to go when we communicated to the entire organization on July 1.

After the company hit "go" on July 1, not everything went perfectly, of course—some things needed to be detailed further or changed. That's when it was so important to listen to the tens of thousands of people on the front line who were starting to live the new model.

Hodson recounts, "We had a live Q&A system up and running. We had a daily huddle with the core team to go through the issues that were being raised. We had a team of people from different parts of the business to which we handed them off. We did a lot of deep listening tours in all of the areas to find out what was landing well versus not and making sure that we were very action-oriented where things weren't going according to plan."

Reengineering the DNA of Your Organization to Focus It on Outcomes

As illustrated by the Microsoft and Honeywell examples, making this capabilities-based organization work can't be achieved by simply changing the lines and boxes on your organization chart—you will likely need to modify and even reengineer the DNA of your organization to make it much more collaborative and to focus it more on outcomes. Beyond the work of architecting and blueprinting the critical outcome-oriented teams, there are four enablers we've seen leaders emphasize the most because they can make or break your effort to re-architect the organization: the way you allocate investments and budgets; how you define, measure and reward performance; how you set up career paths; and how you evolve your culture by encouraging new behaviors.

Reshape Your Planning and Budgeting Process to Allocate Investments to What Drives Your Advantage

To make the capabilities-based organization work, you will need to rethink how you allocate budgets and investments and how you manage the P&L. That is one of the most powerful levers leaders have to focus the company's activities on what matters most. Given how critical the differentiating capabilities are for your organization's success, the bulk of your spending will need to go into building and scaling up those capabilities. And since outcome-oriented teams are the main driver behind your company's differentiating capabilities, the bulk of your investment needs to be directed toward those teams. In fact, we would argue that if you haven't substantially reallocated investments and if your budgets have changed only minimally, you are likely investing in your past more than you are in your future.

This will have potentially significant consequences for how the P&L is managed and for your planning processes. Instead of functional leaders dictating exactly how many people they need and what tools they need to invest in, your outcome-oriented teams must make choices on the investments they need and what they need the functions to deliver for them. At the same time, functional excellence requirements will have to be considered based on the minimum quality standards, budgets, and plans of the outcome-oriented teams. Similarly, your outcome-oriented teams will need to define requirements and targets for business units to take into account during their planning activities (and vice versa). This shift in planning and budget management from the traditional matrix organization will require a rethink of the planning processes and mechanisms that enable governance and collaboration. Who leads the planning cycle, how budgets get finalized, who participates in business reviews during the year, and how decisions get made across the organization will all need to be reset to support the working of your new model. To free up the resources required for the organization's differentiating capabilities, you will need to be ruthless in areas that should be "lights on" (which are necessary but which you should spend as little as possible on) and table stakes (where you need to be as good as competitors but not better). The change will likely require iteration and fine-tuning to bring along the required balance of power within the organization toward teams that truly collaborate to achieve value-creating outcomes.

Redesign How You Define, Measure, and Reward Performance

To shift the focus of the organization toward building and scaling your differentiating capabilities, you will need to change the organization's metrics to the outcomes you want to achieve. What metrics are appropriate depends on your specific situation. It could be time-to-market for new innovations, carbon footprint and sustainability impact, customer satisfaction, the impact you're having on the success of the ecosystem as a whole, or (as in Microsoft's case) customers' consumption of services (a measure of whether customers are experiencing outcomes). One of the major changes Microsoft made was how it compensates its people. It's no more about the value of the contract, but the customer's consumption over time. The company measures consumption for all its customers, which enables leaders to engage individual salespeople in a discussion about the obstacles they face to get their customer to move forward. What Microsoft did—and what any company must do that aims to bring the capabilities-based organization to life—was to measure performance and compensate people based on specific outcomes, not on output.

Some organizations, like law firms and consulting firms, are even linking employee bonus incentives to the results their customers achieve. Instead of measuring and paying people solely based on how much revenue they generate, the firms include whether their clients achieved the results sought. These incentives require careful calibration, as client results may not accrue within the typical annual performance appraisal cycle. However, such incentives create a powerful mechanism to focus the organization on collaborating to achieve truly value-creating outcomes.

You will also need to rethink the balance of individual incentives versus team incentives. Most incentives today relate to selling products or services, and therefore get to a single point of accountability quickly: Did the person hit their sales quota? Did the leader deliver on their commitment? While those incentives are important, you will also need to make sure that you make progress in building and deploying your company's fundamental advantage—its capabilities system. This requires meaningful teaming between outcome-oriented teams, functions, and business units that must embrace, incorporate, improve, and integrate this advantage. Those team-based objectives and incentives need to be established—and appropriately balanced with expectations for individual performance and behaviors—for your transformation to be successful.

You will also need to change how you do performance reviews, who participates in these reviews, and the type of conversation in that review. As part of Microsoft's journey to adopt a capabilities-based organization model, Courtois killed their traditional midyear review, which he found not to be in line with the company's new way of working. Not only did it cause leaders to spend too much time away from the market and away from customers, it had also resulted in lecturing and finger-pointing if an area's performance was lagging. Courtois replaced that with a quarterly business connect in which the team has a shared dialogue around business trends, obstacles and issues, major insights, and what they as a team need to do to succeed. The focus of the discussion became more about the collective actions to take to achieve results and the help needed. Since your company's ability to create lasting value depends on delivering integrated outcomes, you too will need to shift your performance dialogues to focus on collaborative outcomes.

Put in Place Career Models That Make the Fluid Organization a Reality

The traditional hierarchical development models of the past, where people spend their entire career in a function and move up through a series of vertical promotions, aren't what is needed today. To deliver the critical cross-functional capabilities that enable your place in the world, you will need employees who have both deep experiences *within* their area of specialization and diverse experiences *across* areas. This depth and breadth of experiences is also increasingly what employees are looking for to keep their skills relevant and preserve multiple career options in the midst of a rapidly changing business landscape. We already see this model in many organizations in specific areas, and, in fact, today's senior leadership teams have more diverse experiences than decades ago, reflecting not only the increased prevalence of this career track, but its ability to create great leaders.

This type of interdisciplinary model may not be right for your entire organization, but companies must articulate a set of new career paths and development options to help people build the skills they need. In these new paths, people progress in a series of lateral moves through a number of different functions and teams. They don't have to be managers and leaders to grow; playing the role of a contributor on a team also lets people grow. People can also play the role of a "translator"—someone who facilitates the collaboration between outcome-oriented teams, functions, and business units using their influence rather than positional authority. In this new type of career model, people are not judged and rewarded based on managing an increasing number of internal resources but based on their contribution to the team and the outcomes they are accountable for. In rare instances, people even spend a portion of their careers working with ecosystem partners and developing experiences outside the company. Some companies have institutionalized this development process by creating secondment programs to send key talent to work for partner organizations for a time before returning to their "home" organization—and we expect more companies to send employees to partners as we integrate capabilities and need to ensure trust and seamlessness in service of an ecosystem's role in society. In sum, in the capabilities-based organization, career paths also need to be designed from an outcome-oriented mindset—focused on whatever is necessary to get the best outcomes, rather than based on a traditional view of organization hierarchy.

Michael Corbat, the former CEO of Citigroup, relates to this. In the old days, he says, "people were used to running their professional lives in relatively narrow verticals, being responsible for optimizing a vertical, and ascending in their vertical." But creating the best-in-life experiences that Citigroup aims to offer their customers (see chapter 2) requires the company to stitch together many different capabilities. People now progress through many lateral moves that allow them to gain much broader experiences and collaboration skills. "There are no more straight lines to a job. We give people a more curated journey of their career," Corbat adds.

Given the variety and complexity of career paths as we move into a world beyond digital, people will need more one-on-one career coaching and mentoring. There's no longer a single highway that leads upward; there are many different roads with many lateral moves. Some of the steps you should consider:

- Build into your career model an understanding that people do not need to have positional authority or manage large teams to grow and develop. Career advancement and the related growth in financial rewards can happen via working across a number of roles, teams, and experiences.

- Encourage people to take risks and step into careers outside of their traditional functional expertise and training. Give them the support to make these changes.

- Set up talent review processes that are explicitly cross-boundary and enable explicit choices on what else people can do outside the teams they know and currently work in. Talent processes also need to include opportunities for people to go work with ecosystem partners, customers, and others to develop experience that is valued within the organization.

- Help people develop the skills they need to thrive in this new environment (for more on the upskilling imperative, see chapter 7).

Facilitate the Change by Shaping New Behaviors

Asking people to work in this new capabilities-based model is a huge shift. They will have to let go of traditional functional loyalties and priorities to reorient their thinking around a new outcome—which in many cases will be continuously innovated and shifted over time. They will have to learn new skills that may be alien to them, or for which they may have relied on someone else in the past. This time, they will not be able to rely on someone in IT to run data analysis for them—they will instead have to learn how to do it on the fly and apply their expertise to it. Traditional power and decision-making structures will change around them, and they will have to learn how to achieve an outcome by working with and through others instead of being able to rely on their individual efforts. The mindset and behavior changes needed will very likely be significant and possibly even unnatural and unsettling.

Formal measures like changing budgets, metrics, and incentives will help, but you won't succeed in "un-training" and retraining people to work in the new way without explicitly helping them shape and practice new behaviors. In other words, you will need a grease to help the organization work in the ways needed and to shape the culture that reinforces your value creation system.

When articulating the behaviors you want people to adopt, ensure that they are specific, visible, actionable, emotionally resonant, and, ideally, motivating. Depending on your specific situation, the key could be behaviors like fostering explicit conversations about trade-offs between quality, speed, and budget; giving expert input freely and willingly (but if someone decides to go another way, supporting them); making decisions and articulating the facts behind decisions clearly; and aligning resources explicitly to prioritized opportunities to maximize impact.

For Microsoft's commercial transformation program to be successful, leaders knew they had to define what that new selling approach should be, and measure, wherever possible, whether the organization was moving in the right direction. They were quite granular in their definition of the new behaviors they wanted people to exhibit, as Jean-Philippe Courtois explains:

> First, we need our people to engage much more with business decision makers as opposed to IT people—and that is easy to measure. Second, we defined how they should trigger the right conversation once they go to those customer meetings—how they learn from the customers, and how they get relevant by having an intelligent conversation. Third, after they've established the relevance in that first meeting, how do they then point to an engagement model where they're going to bring relevant industry specialists and digital advisors to do some business envisioning together with the customer and develop an agenda of transformation that Microsoft can support? And fourth, how do they then bring our tech person and the customer's tech person together so they translate that into the digital capabilities that we need to build?

This new behavior model was facilitated by a significant investment in training and development and engagement of the organization on how to implement the behaviors in practice.

Eli Lilly illustrates the critical role that leadership plays in enabling those key behaviors and eliminating disincentives and roadblocks (we will tell Eli Lilly's transformation story in more detail in chapter 6). For Lilly's transformation to be successful, one of the most important imperatives was to speed up the company's innovation process. This required formal changes in the organization and in leadership roles, such as giving the heads of its five new business units more involvement and more decision rights in the later stages of R&D. But it also required people to change how they behaved. "Resistance to change is particularly strong at Lilly because Lilly is the largest and most attractive employer in the region, and there are few alternatives," says Dan Skovronsky, who co-led the R&D overhaul. "People are afraid of taking risks because losing your job may mean packing up your family and moving. So why try and chase things? It's better just to keep your head down and keep working here, because it's such a nice place to work."

Resistance to change, however, was the failure mode, given that the company needed to develop and bring new drugs to market much faster than had been the practice in the past. Traditionally, the environment it had created was one where the most important thing was for you to hit the deadlines you said you were going to hit, which led people to create generously buffered deadlines, which in turn led Lilly to be among the slowest in the industry. Says Skovronsky,

> We needed to set ambitious goals and not penalize people when they failed to hit them. We had to give employees the confidence that they're not going to lose their job, that they were not going to get demoted because they took a risk and it didn't work out. We needed to show them that, in fact, that was the route to promotion. We told them, "Forget about the buffer. Give me the really aggressive best-in-industry timeline. Tell me what you need to achieve that, and don't be afraid if you miss it by a couple of weeks or a couple of months. The fact that you tried to do something really bold means you're still going to be way better than you would have been before." We had examples of teams that missed their deadlines, but they had incredibly aggressive, unbuffered, best-in-class type of deadlines. They were two months late, but two years faster

than they would have been in the old system. We rewarded them, made heroes out of them, and did storytelling around them. And that, I would say—more than anything else—was what was required to make the change happen.

While these may be nice stories, shaping the right behaviors that lead to the outcomes you want takes real work. It is a strategic exercise and effort not to be left to chance, or to the HR department to solve. Years of research and work in this area tells us that shaping behaviors requires defining the few critical behaviors you want to see manifested in your organization and assiduously cultivating them.[1]

There is no one-size-fits-all answer to the perfect key behaviors. However, the work of the Katzenbach Center at PwC's Strategy&, a global knowledge center on culture and leadership, has taught us that critical behaviors can be shaped with a few simple steps:

- Inventory and understand the existing cultural traits and behaviors of the organization in a neutral way—realizing that your current behaviors will have both positive and negative implications. Assess how your existing culture supports and hinders your strategy. (For more information, see the Katzenbach Center's Culture Thumbprint Survey.[2])

- Engage people to understand what specific behaviors are needed to support your new way of working and your new model of value creation. Be specific: What does it look like? What does it feel like? Where do you already see those behaviors in action?

- Get people to identify what's getting in the way of demonstrating that behavior. What practices can be adopted to put the behavior in place? What enablers would help? What roadblocks need to be removed?

- Make it real. Put enablers in place and remove obstacles. Give role models a platform to spread the behaviors. Engage people to translate behaviors into specific actions relevant to their day-to-day jobs and tie them directly to the strategic objectives. What does it mean to collaborate in finance versus sales? What behaviors can leaders and supervisors focus on that will motivate frontline workers to adjust their behavior? Keep refining the behaviors to make them real.[3]

. . .

Establishing a capabilities-based organization is a great goal but naturally involves intrusive change in all the areas we've highlighted—structure, budgeting and planning, performance management, career paths, and how people behave—all of which are related. In many cases, you will need to rethink and even undo basic ways your company has worked. It is for this reason that we see many companies making this journey in steps, introducing select outcome-oriented teams before migrating the entire organization structure. This gives time to mature people processes, governance processes, and other important enablers to enable the capabilities-based organization to work.

The rationale for change to the organization, however, is inescapable. When the fundamental model for how you create value changes, the organization must change. The transformation needs to bring capabilities and outcomes to the surface and make them the primary focus of the organization. This won't be easy. Defenses in the old organization will be activated. But the change is critical. Your top team will therefore have to embrace it wholeheartedly. And the top team itself will have to change, as we will see in the next chapter.

6

Invert the Focus of Your Leadership Team

We may have all come on different ships, but we're
in the same boat now.

—Martin Luther King Jr.

When Eli Lilly unveiled a massive transformation effort in 2009 in
the midst of plunging profitability, the headline news was that the
pharma giant, founded in 1876, was recommitting to its historical
purpose: creating therapies and cures that make life better for people
around the world. Lilly referred to its situation as the "Years YZ" crisis. This was a reference to an earlier tough time known internally as
"Year X"—that was 2001, when the patent on Prozac, the company's
blockbuster antidepressant drug, had run out. In 2009, Lilly was facing an even bigger challenge, as patent protection was about to
expire on four drugs that accounted for 40 percent of the company's
revenue. Institutional investors were skeptical about the transformation plan, but Lilly stated that it would not seek a "mega-merger" with
another pharma company or reduce R&D spending, as several of its

global rivals were doing. Then-CEO John Lechleiter said, "We are going to innovate our way out of this problem."

Dave Ricks, the current CEO, explains: "The bet was about our own innovation. There is nothing as good as this business if you can invent a new substance that can affect the arc of human health. That's the best business in the world—and when you do it well, it also creates a lot of noneconomic value everywhere."

That the company was recommitting to its historical identity doesn't mean that it did not have to transform. On the contrary. The company's late-stage innovation pipeline was running dry; R&D efforts were unfocused; time-to-market was one of the slowest in the industry; too many decisions were delegated up to the CEO; incentives were misaligned; and costs were out of control, especially given the looming drop in revenue. Lechleiter, the CEO who would be responsible for transforming the company, had been COO for three years before moving into the top job in early 2008, so he was fully aware of the severity of the situation. In fact, the previous CEO had retired early to leave his successor enough time to find a solution.[1]

Key to the transformation that Lilly was going to undertake was a change in operating model and a drastic repositioning of Lilly's top leadership team. Lechleiter created five business units—diabetes, oncology, biomedicines, emerging markets, and animal health—instead of relying on the company's previous functional model. This change was meant to enable more collaboration focused on specific health outcomes in each of those therapeutic areas. The change also allowed for faster decision-making that focused more on customers. In addition, the company created a Development Center of Excellence to increase the speed and efficiency of the development of new products.

The top team underwent massive change, too. Up until 2009, the top team was known as the Policy Committee, and nine of the thirteen members represented functions, while only three—the heads of Research & Development, Manufacturing & Quality, and Global

Pharma operations—had operational responsibilities. The imbalance seemed to be both a symptom and a cause of the strategic and operational shortcomings that had led to the YZ crisis. In line with the new operating model, Lechleiter set up a newly named Executive Committee and added the heads of the five new business units to the team, while reducing the number of leaders with functional responsibilities to five. Overall, eight of the thirteen members of the Executive Committee were new to that team, and two had been hired from the outside.

The change in the committee's focus and energy was dramatic. "The dynamic completely flipped," says Stephen Fry, head of HR. "On the old committee, the majority of people believed their job was to be the checks and balances to people who were actually leading the business. The new committee had a majority of people who had P&Ls and operational responsibility, and the discussion in the room became much more business-execution-oriented, and that led to an ability to execute like we had never executed before."

The mix of backgrounds of the top team members also changed dramatically, creating a powerful combination. Lechleiter had a background in science and deep experience in drug development, which positioned him well to lead the push for more innovation. The business unit presidents had extensive commercialization experience. They were chosen for their political skills, their ability to balance decisiveness with the loss of power experienced by others, and their deep understanding of the entire value chain that would help them drive commercial success. "We're fortunate that we had people who were ready to take on these roles, particularly since we had been accustomed to developing people to lead functional areas like sales and marketing, not to run a whole business," commented Mark Ferrara, vice president of Talent Management.[2]

Lechleiter was looking for leaders who could shake things up—especially around innovation—and found one in Daniel Skovronsky, who had joined the company in 2010 when Lilly acquired Avid

Radiopharmaceuticals, which he had founded six years earlier. He had no experience in Big Pharma and, initially a skeptic about the YZ transformation, he looked at Lilly's R&D operations with fresh eyes. Eighteen months into the next-generation development initiative, the team tasked with significantly reducing time to market of new drugs held one of its quarterly updates to the CEO. "I raised my hand," Skovronsky recalls, "and said, 'So, if I understand your presentation correctly, you're saying our goal is to be among the slowest in the industry, and we're not achieving that goal?' That was a very disruptive thing to say and led to me getting a job to be one of the people to help fix the problem."

Lechleiter, indeed, chose Skovronsky as one of two leaders of what became a highly successful transformation of the company's innovation activities. "One lesson I learned was, don't complain about something unless you want to be the guy to fix it," Skovronsky says. Today, Skovronsky is Lilly's chief scientific officer and president of Lilly Research Laboratories and also has responsibility for global business development.

Skovronsky remembers the CEO giving him a piece of paper on which he had typed up a couple of things about what was wrong with development at Lilly: "I still have that paper folded up in my desk. John [Lechleiter] asked me not to show it to anyone, so I haven't shown it to anyone. But it became my blueprint for shaking things up. In a way it was obvious stuff, but it was important for me to have that mandate from the CEO to change things." He adds, "We probably don't tell people very often, 'You're here to shake it up.'"

Lechleiter worked hard to find the right balance between having business unit presidents focus on managing their own units and having the top team drive the agenda of the company together. Because business units faced very different situations—emerging markets were still experiencing strong growth, whereas biomedicines needed deep restructuring, since that's where almost all patent expirations were going to hit—it was important to have some leaders focused on growing their businesses while others could focus on turnaround. Getting the balance right helped the team increase the speed and customer focus of decision making: while Lechleiter was still the decision maker for key operating questions, he was no longer the single point at which all business unit decisions were made. To make sure that leaders "put team Lilly before their own unit," explains Fry, "we kept executive incentives linked to total performance rather than business unit results. That helped leaders make the right execution decisions consistent with our strategy."

At the same time, Lilly changed the physical layout of the offices at headquarters. "There were some thirty corporate people sitting together," says Fry,

> The BU heads sat with operations, manufacturing sat somewhere else, the head of R&D went back and forth. The whole place had wood paneling everywhere. Most people had their own toilet in their office. The dynamic was incredible. Someone would tell me, "Tell Mr. X this." And I would say "You sit next to him, why don't you go talk to him?" We no longer have that now. If there's something that needs to happen, we go sort it out. And it was almost an immediate flip. It is amazing how the new top team composition and the physical layout of the offices forced that collaboration.

A key decision on who was going to be responsible for which parts of R&D greatly increased collaboration across the company. The top team had gone on an off-site in 2009 to figure out what to do. Michael Overdorf, Lilly's former chief strategy officer, remembers: "John [Lechleiter] encouraged his direct reports to discuss advantages and disadvantages. There was a full-on debate in the room. And then, at the end, John just said, 'Okay, everybody has poured concrete around their positions, and no one is budging. So this is what I get paid to do. I'm drawing this, and we're done.' And the meeting was over. No more debate. I think John even kept that flip chart. It was his stake in the ground. That was the bet we were going to make."

Lechleiter's decision gave business units responsibility for R&D right after phase 2 (preclinical research)—before that, phase 3 (clinical research) had still been managed by the companywide R&D unit. This significantly changed the dynamics because once business unit leaders owned part of R&D, they got a better appreciation for some of the challenges and the investment needs. It also increased Lilly's focus on commercial impact, pushing leaders to make decisions earlier if they saw that something wasn't going to be a major product. And probably most importantly, it brought shared ownership and accountability. When a business unit leader was forced to decide whether they'd put their next dollar into an R&D project or into preserving a sales rep, the answer would be R&D.

The team needed to take many tough decisions and put many stakes in the ground—and they had many heated debates. Dave Ricks, who had been president of biomedicine before becoming CEO, remembers, "We didn't always see things the same way. In fact, mostly we didn't. One disadvantage of the business unit model is that you naturally see the world through your own lens. Someone running a high-growth business and someone running a shrinking business do see things differently, so there was a natural tension. But I think amongst the inner core group of people, there was not really a doubt that we were going to get this done." Skovronsky adds, "I was skeptical at first. What got me on board, eventually, was the recognition that we had a leadership team that was committed to making this strategy work, and that, with the right people and the right resources, we would actually be able to execute on our innovation strategy."

As the initial transformation plan promised, Lilly continued to invest in R&D. Between 2007 and 2016, R&D spending as a percentage of sales increased from 19 percent to 25 percent, and the pipeline began to generate new drugs—ten launches in five years. "They're not all great," says Skovronsky, "but six or seven will be blockbusters, and that doesn't happen by chance. That's the result of a systematic approach to building an innovation capability."

By 2016, with its revivified R&D operations, refocused organizational structure and leadership team, and leaner footprint, Lilly was firmly back on a path of profitable growth. Over the next five years, the stock price tripled. Fry reflects on the impact of the transformation: "I think all the foundation for who we are today was set during YZ. Sticking to that innovation strategy against all the external advice allowed us to have the hand of cards that we now have. And so I think today's success was all built on that transformation."

Transforming will require you, like Lilly, to address your leadership team—who's on it, what they focus on, and how they lead. Just as your company needs a strategic effort to build the right differentiating capabilities to create value, your team will need to build the leadership competencies needed to enable this new form of value creation. (See "Is Your Leadership Team *Leading*?")

Working in a capabilities-based way is not how most leaders have grown up—and the transition isn't going to be easy. That's why you will need to carefully consider what kind of leadership competencies you really need. And your leadership team will need help managing the many demands of your current businesses while also negotiating the major choices and changes in behavior needed to create value in the future.

Our research identified three significant actions that help leadership teams drive the transformation to a digitally powered, capabilities-driven organization:

- **Establish the top team required to shape your future.** Your reimagined place in the world requires you to rethink what roles, skills, and backgrounds are needed to deliver the capabilities you've chosen to focus on. What roles do you need to balance traditional business units and functions with the new capability-aligned and outcome-oriented teams? Who

Is Your Leadership Team *Leading*?

We like to challenge leadership teams to think through whether they spend their time together really *leading* the company. Consider the following questions to judge whether you and your team make the most of your time together to position your company for success:

- How much of your time is spent on running the day-to-day versus shaping the future?

- How much of your time is spent reacting to what the organization brings versus what the leadership team should be driving?

- How often do your strategic discussions lead you to making the hard choices about your company's future?

- When your team spends time on strategy, do you focus on the external environment or the bold choices that your organization must make?

- How much time is spent on reviews of actions after the fact versus on proactively shaping actions and a direction?

---

can help you get insight into the key issues from a market, customer and technology perspective? Who can challenge your thinking and bring in new perspectives needed to reimagine the future?

- **Shift your leadership team's focus toward driving the transformation, not just responding to today's demands.** Your leadership team will need to fully own and embrace the transformation. At the same time, it has to keep the organization

- How often do you ask people to come back with more detailed proposals because your team doesn't quite have the energy or the clear vision that allows you to be decisive?

- How often do you spend time discussing in whose area of responsibility an issue falls and who should go tackle it?

- How often do you work together with your colleagues on an issue?

- How well do you know your colleagues in your leadership team? Do you get the feeling that your colleagues care about your success, and do you care about theirs?

You may be surprised by the result. Some teams find that more than half of their time is spent in rather unproductive ways; but much more importantly, they find they aren't dedicating the energy to the transformation that will position them for success in the beyond digital age.

focused to deliver today. What structures and mechanisms will allow you to ensure the urgent does not overwhelm the important?

- **Take ownership for how your leadership team collaborates and behaves.** With creating value in the beyond digital world requiring such a high degree of collaboration, your own behaviors will need explicit attention and care so you can build the culture that will inspire your organization's collective success.

You will certainly have to work on these areas simultaneously, as they reinforce each other. You may not get everything perfectly right on the first take, including how you establish the team itself. This will take effort and may be a focus for some time, as a high-performing leadership team will make the journey ahead much more inspiring and impactful.

Establish Your Top Team Based on the Right Skills Mix

The first task is to take a hard look at whether you actually have the right team for the job that needs to be done. When you look at the capabilities that you need to leverage, enhance, or build, you will probably conclude that you need to add nontraditional leadership roles to your team (and likely eliminate some older ones). In fact, we have seen an explosion of C-suite titles and new roles in recent years. Think about *chief innovation officers* who lead teams of people with backgrounds in R&D, engineering, marketing, customer insights, product management, and IT to improve how a company launches products or services. Or, *chief quality officers* or *chief sustainability officers* who change how work is done across all company functions. Or, *chief analytics officers*, *chief behavioral officers*, *chief brand officers*, *chief customer officers*, and *chief design officers*. What's important, however, is not the titles, but that these roles focus on building and scaling up the capabilities required to deliver on your value proposition, rather than on running traditional single functions or P&Ls. Some companies have taken first steps in this direction, but, in many organizations, these roles don't go far enough and don't translate into the outcomes-oriented organization we discussed in the last chapter. If building customer relationships is a capability on which you seek to differentiate yourself, you may need a role on the leadership team that can own how you manage the entire life cycle of a customer's experience—not a person who is responsible for the selling or customer service processes.

You will also need to incorporate your ecosystem in your new set of roles. In the old world, where ecosystem was often equated with suppliers, the head of procurement was usually in charge of bringing potential issues to the attention of the top team. In this ecosystem-enabled era, however, your leadership roles need to map to responsibility for capabilities, both inside the organization and outside your own four walls in the larger ecosystem. Microsoft, for example, put in place a Corporate Vice President, One Commercial Partner, to simplify the engagement between partners and Microsoft's own sales organization and to enable partners to effectively serve customers.[2] This isn't just a fancy title. The creation of such a very senior role reflects the importance of the ecosystem to the execution of the company's value proposition and ensures that the ecosystem is represented in decision making.

Getting to a capabilities-based leadership model does not have to be done in one shot via a major reorganization; however, one of the most frequent mistakes leaders talk about is not moving fast enough on key positions. Some roles can work as part of a transition, but the more that roles are aligned to your reimagined place, the better. And if you conclude that you need a chief digital officer or chief analytics officer for a transition period, make sure you don't set them up as "pirate ships" that exist outside the core structure for building and exploiting your capabilities—but integrate them tightly with the actual work of your company.

Leaders often struggle to remove scope from an existing leader— new capability roles wind up being too weak to drive transformation, or there are simply too many roles to allow for clear accountability. Your leadership team should reflect the balance of the new organizational construct we described in the last chapter—market- and customer-facing P&Ls, strong cross-functional teams based on capabilities and oriented to outcomes, and narrower functional areas.

The roles you choose to have on your leadership team send a signal to the organization, to customers, to your ecosystem partners, to investors, and to potential employees about the strategic destination you have chosen and about how you are transforming to achieve that future. Apple's creation of the chief design officer position in 2015, for example, signaled to the organization (and, in fact, the world) the outstanding importance that design has for Apple and helped make the point that it is an organizational capability, not just a trait of the founder's genius. Creating the role greatly helped Apple attract the world's best designers, from the fashion industry and elsewhere, and produced one of the most differentiating capabilities that Apple ever built.

Once you've determined the roles you need on your leadership team, you can proceed to filling them with the right people. You will most certainly need leaders who have a deep understanding of what technology can do for you, and you will need leaders who have different backgrounds, experiences, and ways of working than those you may have traditionally sought.

In the past, leaders often hired chief information officers because they felt uncomfortable dealing with technology. Leaders were "outsourcing" the company's digital challenges and opportunities. It should be obvious by now that this isn't a sustainable model. Given how central technology is to your value creation, *every* leader needs to embrace digital. Every leader needs to understand how technology is changing the world around them; and how they can use technology to improve what they offer customers; how they develop, produce, and deliver products and services; how they engage customers, and so on, so that their company can deliver on its future place in the world. Not every leader will need to be able to program a bot, and not everyone on your team will need to be a digital native—

though you may need a few of those, too—but having that under-standing of what technology can do—and do for your capabilities, in particular—is a prerequisite for every successful leader today. What does that mean for people on your current team who do *not* have that technology understanding? We'd argue that if they don't recognize the need to become digitally savvy and show no interest in develop-ing that skill set, then they may not be the leaders who will lead your company to a successful future.

Digital savvy, of course, is not all you need in your leaders. As described in chapter 5, the capabilities-based organization you are building is inherently more complex and integrated than the tradi-tional functional model most companies have relied on in the past. You will need leaders with a broad range of skills, experiences and perspectives to make this organization work. You will need people who can see problems and opportunities from a completely different angle. You will therefore need to seek people who look, think, feel, and act differently than your organization does today and be open to—and encourage—being challenged. What all this adds up to is that you will need a much more diverse set of leaders to lead you through this transformation.

There is ample evidence that diverse teams perform better.[3] Researchers at the University of Michigan, for example, found that diverse groups can solve problems better than a more homogenous team of greater objective ability.[4]

However, what we're talking about here goes beyond the typical corporate diversity initiatives—we challenge you to be strategic about the backgrounds and experiences you seek so that the leader-ship team represents the future the company is transforming to. You will need team members with experiences in different fields, who have worked with different ecosystems, and who understand the different capabilities, technologies, channels, and transformational approaches you will be deploying. You will need leaders who have demonstrated that they can build and scale up the capabilities you are seeking to perfect. Industry boundaries are blurring, and you need leaders with the best talents, regardless of the industry in which they gained their core experiences. For example, the health-care industry is rapidly morphing into an amalgam of traditional health care, consumer products, and Silicon Valley high-tech companies as the field becomes more personalized and technology-enabled. This means challenging traditional thinking with capabilities from the traditional B2C consumer products and retail domain and marrying those strengths with the technical innovation of designers from Silicon Valley. It's not easy to find a single individual who can blend all these capabilities, so you often have to bring people with different backgrounds, life experiences, and skills together and help them harmonize into a single chorus. The very nature of the transformation ahead calls for a bold group that will challenge each other with new ideas and thinking, and diversity is becoming table stakes in our view if you want to solve tomorrow's challenges.

You also need to seek out team members whose experiences reflect the diverse voices of your total ecosystem—including the customers you will be seeking to serve, your workforce, and your partners. Very likely, these voices will include different gender identities; national, racial, and ethnic backgrounds; abilities; and economic and educational backgrounds. Some companies have even started to include leaders from some of their ecosystem partners into their management committees, to more meaningfully engage with those partners.

Here's how Carla Kriwet, former chief business leader of Connected Care at Philips, described her leadership team:

> Sixty percent of my leadership team is new. We have many positions that didn't exist before, like the innovation leader or the marketing leader at cluster level, or the chief medical officer or the Connected Care communication leader. We now have twelve different nationalities on my team. It sometimes feels like the United Nations, but I think it's critically impor-

tant because health-care systems are so different across countries. If you have a team full of Americans who think of Europe like one US state, that won't work because health-care systems and reimbursement models are very different. If you only have Europeans, and they don't understand how the large hospital chains in the US work and what their issues are around cybersecurity and safety, that won't work either. I need people on my leadership team who naturally can connect. And therefore, one of the top requirements for people to join my leadership team was that they needed to have lived in different countries. Not to have had a production site in China among their responsibilities, or to know a supplier in India, but to actually have lived there so they know what the cultural differences mean.

You will also need to actively look for leaders on your team who exhibit the behaviors you have defined as critical: people who know how to lead via influence and encouragement rather than relying on their positional authority; people who are not concerned with the power, size, and budget of their areas but are instead focused on delivering outcomes; people who have the courage to acknowledge that they do not have all the answers and instead seek answers from their teams; people who can truly engage others around the purpose of what you're trying to achieve, and people whose purpose is as much tied to delivering incredible outcomes as it may be to achieving their own personal success. Perhaps this could mean that your next leader will be a former ninth-grade teacher who had to manage an unruly classroom, or a pastor who had to listen to the complaints and worries of parishioners and help them chart a path forward. The leader of the future does not have to be cut from a single cloth from an MBA or engineering school.

To be clear, we aren't suggesting running a corporate diversity initiative that makes for a colorful page in your annual report or making these changes out of purely altruistic motives or a sense of social commitment. Those motives may form a part of your thinking (and we would strongly encourage you to include them). But you need to be equally clear that you are creating voices for your much more complex ecosystem and putting together the best team with a mix of sensibilities who will help enrich your capabilities system.

As Hitachi, for example, started transforming from a diverse product-driven conglomerate into a solutions provider focused on social innovation businesses to create value (see chapter 2), top leaders realized they would need to completely reconfigure Hitachi's leadership team, aiming for more diversity and types of experience. To lead the transformation, they brought in a new set of executives with restructuring expertise, external perspective, and the willingness to sacrifice sacred cows. "What your team has to do is to introduce more diversity in the Executive Committee," Chief Strategy Officer Mamoru Morita recalls then-CEO Takashi Kawamura saying. "Look at the makeup of the Executive Committee right now. They're all in their fifties or sixties and have worked at Hitachi their whole lives. They all think the same way and say the same things. That's where things go wrong." So Hitachi brought in new talent. Nakanishi, for example, who succeeded Kawamura as president, and later as CEO, had a wider set of experiences than most Hitachi executives; he had earned a master's degree in computer engineering at Stanford and been away from headquarters for several years, working first as head of Hitachi Europe, then Hitachi Global Storage Technologies in the United States. Although Hitachi's leadership team is still dominated by Japanese executives, several non-Japanese executives were appointed to senior roles. Alistair Dormer, from the United Kingdom, was named executive officer of the railway systems business in 2015 and later became EVP leading the mobility sector. In 2018, Brice Koch, from Switzerland, was named president and CEO of Hitachi Automotive Systems (Hitachi Astemo since 2021).

Hitachi puts a lot of emphasis on becoming more attractive as an employer for non-Japanese managers. Its 2020 acquisition of ABB Power Grids under CEO Toshiaki Higashihara was an important milestone. "With the addition of ABB's thirty-six thousand power-grid employees, Hitachi now has more non-Japanese than Japanese employees in the group," says Morita. "It will give Hitachi opportunities to accumulate global business experience and will give all employees much greater opportunities for thinking with a global mindset in day-to-day operations. Global job opportunities for our employees will be much more plentiful, which is good for people development."

Shift Your Leadership Team's Focus toward Driving the Transformation, Not Just Responding to Today's Demands

A CEO once described a fundamental shift they made in how they managed their work: "I used to spend all of my time responding to other people's issues—through email, meetings, the entire day was making decisions related to what others provided. One day, I recognized that the only way to lead the company was to do the work I feel was required for the organization to move forward."

Time is the top team's scarcest resource. What is the top team going to focus on, and how is it going to make sure that the urgent does not overtake the important? Given the amount of change ahead of you, it is even more important now for your leadership team to be very deliberate about how it sets its agenda to make sure it drives the transformation, rather than let the agenda be driven by requests coming from the organization.

Leadership teams will always need to manage two distinct agendas: running the business on a day-to-day, quarter-by-quarter basis and building for the future that you've committed to. Philips's CEO Frans van Houten explains: "We talk about the need to both 'perform and transform.' If you only transform but don't perform, you have no here-and-now. If you only perform but don't transform, you have no future. Therefore, in our scorecards we measure both. In our reviews, we talk about both. And the targets that I give to all my executives, there are always some transform objectives."

Top team members need to put sufficient horsepower around each of these goals to make sure the longer-term questions don't fall prey to the short-term need for firefighting. Some companies create a separate group to manage a strategic transformation distinct from operations. Usually, these groups share many members and may even include individuals who aren't part of the top team to infuse new thinking. However, even in these cases, the top team is still accountable for the transformation and for the performance of the transformation team.

The topics you'll need to work through can be structured along the imperatives described in this book: you will need to reimagine your company's place in the world, determine how to build privileged insights into the customers you care about, develop your ecosystems, re-architect your organization and culture to deliver business outcomes, reposition your leadership team, and reinvent the social contract with your people.

Setting the agenda of the team is one of the most important levers for the CEO. That's why CEOs will not want to delegate agenda setting but rather drive the thinking behind this important task. Make room to think boldly about the future *and* translate that thinking into the everyday. Some companies make reviewing the progress in building the company's differentiating capabilities a standing item on their meeting agenda, reflecting its importance and complexity. Others have separate, periodic meetings focused solely on the transformation.

Frans van Houten considered the organization of his Executive Committee off-site meetings so important that he took care of it himself. Recalls CFO Abhijit Bhattacharya, "There's of course a lot of preparation required for those top team off-sites. For the first two boot camps, Frans drove the whole preparation of the entire trip himself. There's no external agency involved; we only have one facilitator who watches us and gives us input in case we are missing something. The program is really leader-led—it's a huge investment we make."

Your role as a member of the leadership team does not stop with making these big choices about differentiation—you will also need to make sure that these important choices get executed. You will need to get your hands dirty working through the details of how to implement the various measures and how to make sure that what the organization builds adds up to a coherent whole.

Finally, you should hold yourself and your team accountable to spending the time and energy leading the way ahead. Consider metrics as simple as how much of your senior leadership agenda is spent on the strategic and transformational topics, or you can pulse the organization more broadly to gauge their independent perspective for how well you as a team are driving forward. Such tools and insights help ensure that you make the most of your leadership team.

Take Ownership for How Your Leadership Team Collaborates and Behaves

As part of having reimagined your company's place in the world, you will have identified a significant problem your company is going to help solve. Resolving such a massive problem can't be driven by one or two people only—it requires a level of shared accountability and collaboration that most companies do not have today.

Most companies typically experience a lot of competition in their top ranks: competition for the top job in some cases, but more often just competition for who's managing the strongest P&L or whose function contributes most to those P&Ls. This individualist thinking, while rewarded in many modern corporations because it drives individual accountability, won't help you transform your company. But once leadership teams recognize the magnitude of the task ahead and once they have the individuals who can think in the new way, collaboration becomes much easier. You therefore must get everyone on the top team aligned around an understanding of why your company needs to change, the place in the world you're aiming for, and the differentiating capabilities you will need to get there. Everyone on the team needs to wholeheartedly own the transformation program and see their personal objectives and agendas tied to its success.

What if some people can't seem to get on board? They either need to get on board quickly, or the ship needs to sail without them. As Eli Lilly's Stephen Fry remembers, "There were a few people we had to let go, people who were completely opposed to the new way of running the company, who were completely opposed to the idea of business units because it was taking away part of their power. Letting those leaders go was critical for us being able to get on with the business units having more decision-making input and accountability."

Creating ownership around the vision isn't enough. You must then create a shared purpose for your leadership team. Have them define their remit: Why does the team exist? What big issues are they here to solve? When defining that remit, the team will need to be convinced—or will need to convince themselves—that their most important task is to lead the company through this transformation and that success will depend on the collaboration of team members rather than on the sum of individual functions or P&Ls. Top team members also need to align around the fact that they are gathering not to approve or reject proposals that are brought to them, like justices or legislators, but to work as a team of executives to create value as a team.

Philips's CEO Frans van Houten recounts, "I started to take my executive committee to off-sites—you could call them journeys in nature. I had already done that in earlier years, and what I like very much about these kinds of trips is that the egos become a little bit smaller when you're out in the nature. You leave your phones behind. You're forced to actually transact with each other. In the first couple of years, we took the executive committee on these off-sites in order to have the difficult discussions, but also the personal reflections. What are we here to achieve? What does success look like? But also: Why are you here? Do you want to be here? And, if you are here, can you change your tune in how you transact with each other?"

Satya Nadella, who became Microsoft CEO in 2014, was also clear that he needed "the senior leadership team . . . to become a cohesive team that shared a common world-view." As he writes in his book *Hit Refresh*,

> For anything monumental to happen—great software, innovative hardware, or even a sustainable institution—there needs to be one great mind or a set of agreeing minds. I don't mean yes-men and yes-women. Debate and argument are essential. Improving upon each other's ideas is crucial. . . . But there also has to be high-quality agreement. We needed a senior leadership team (SLT) that would lean into each other's problems, promote dialogue, and be effective. We needed everyone to view the SLT as his or her first team, not just another meeting they attended. We needed to be aligned on mission, strategy, and culture.[5]

You will then need to become more specific and work with leadership to define how they need to behave to help the organization transform. Addressing how your team behaves is not about leaders liking each other and agreeing. It is about establishing behaviors that allow everyone to be effective—to put issues on the table, solve problems together, come to decisions quickly, and feel committed to each other's success.

The Covid-19 crisis has reminded leaders across the globe that their leadership teams must be able to act quickly and effectively. The crisis demonstrated that, under immense pressure, these teams can, in fact, step up and lead in collaborative, decisive, outcome-oriented ways. Instead of tasking some committee with developing recommendations for their workforce or their supply chains, they put their collective insights, perspectives, and experiences together and solved those big, truly cross-company issues as *one* team. If any reader has been the victim of a corporate cybercrime, the imperative for leadership to work together and make decisions is similarly obvious. Perhaps leaders so far haven't perceived quite the same urgency around addressing the larger challenges they face in a world moving beyond digital and haven't therefore stepped up to drive the transformation with the same energy, dedication, and rigor.

Philips's leaders stress showcasing the desired behaviors they want to cascade down throughout the organization. Recalls CFO Bhattacharya,

> When we started our culture journey, we said, "Anything that happens in the company is a reflection of the culture we set around the executive committee." The implications of that, in terms of accountability, are huge. For example, when I did my self-evaluation for my midyear performance appraisal, I put myself as "partially meets" on "customer first," not because I don't visit customers or because I fail to follow a customer issue I'm aware of till it's completely resolved. But if I am the CFO and I have influence over IT, global business services, and finance, and it's still difficult for customers to do business

with Philips, then I should take a big part of that responsibility personally. So I put myself as "partially meets." And I did the same for my direct reports as well.

Equally important to defining the right behaviors is creating mechanisms that ensure you're actually going to exhibit them. You have to be deliberate; you can't just leave the mechanisms to chance. Many teams therefore agree to call each other out for doing things they said they were no longer going to do, or explicitly grant each other permission to ask for help.

At Microsoft, Jean-Philippe Courtois recalls, "We are challenging ourselves every day whether we have the growth mindset we need. I tell myself whether I have a fixed mindset or growth mindset, and I know my moments. I try to keep myself honest and to encourage my team pushing me after some pretty bad behavior, to tell me: 'JPC, that was not the best of your growth mindset.'"

Philips's Frans van Houten emphasizes authentic feedback as well:

> During our off-sites, we always do speed-dating around feedback to make sure we give enough feedback and also to show how much fun it is and how much energy you get from it. So, if you have fifteen minutes between the end of the program and dinner start, you will need to look for two people and tell them what you really appreciate and what would help them grow in their role. We said you need to do at least five a day. It's as simple as that. And then you see people actively looking for who they haven't yet talked to. And it gets them into the habit of thinking about what they should tell their colleagues, what they've observed. It really just helps institutionalize feedback a little bit, in a fun way. We all have these forums and overengineered two-pagers. Whereas, very often, that human connection and feedback on one or two essential things is far more important.

Building trust is an essential element of enabling the team's effectiveness. People need a way—even when they don't agree—to have faith in the process and align around the team's decisions. This trust also allows you to build a culture of testing boundaries and "failing fast"—acknowledging that it's okay to fail as long as you learn from it. Building this trust may require you to revisit how you define "success." Is success based on how many people one manages, and on financial and operational results alone? Or are there other measures, like how much you share talent and how much you collaborate? Other companies build trust via top team interventions, wilderness trips, or asking leaders to explicitly work together on particularly challenging and important tasks.

When Frans van Houten became CEO of Philips, he inherited a team where, as he said, "everyone was used to running their own ship. What I needed, however, was an executive committee with interdependent members—not dependent, not independent, but interdependent. We needed to work together and have the right, robust dialogues in order to then reach common conclusions and pursue common goals." Van Houten was one of these true believers in wilderness trips. His CFO, Abhijit Bhattacharya, remembers:

> Frans has taken his Executive Committee on a boot camp every year since 2015. These are not five-star trips—no, they are very basic. You live in tents. You share a room. You are walking in the wilderness for days. They put you physically deep outside your comfort zone, and mentally, as well. The first trip started in Las Vegas. All we were told is "Block that week and buy a plane ticket to Las Vegas." That was all. When we landed, we got a first message saying, "Now find your way to this hotel." And then in the hotel, they took our bags, laptops, phones, everything. Pairs of two of us were given a limousine, we were told to get into the car, and the driver just took you. We went from place to place, with no clue as to what we were going to do and how long it was going to take.

At some point, we all met for dinner. We were back in the hotel past 1 a.m. and found ourselves sharing rooms. These are all small things, but every single step of the way was something that you are not used to.

While all these mechanisms usually do improve collaboration, we've hardly seen a measure as effective as getting pairs of executives to work together on solving corporate-wide issues. After all, the saying goes, "It's easier to act yourself into a new way of thinking than to think yourself into a new way of acting." The executives get to know one another better, learn to better understand the drivers of success and potential limitations of areas outside their daily sphere of influence, and see the power of having different perspectives come together in a true collaborative solution. Then they can share the satisfaction of having solved a big, complicated problem. And you will have no shortage of such challenges as you find your place and transform. Think carefully about which problems can and should be given to small groups of your leaders, bringing both the right skills and an opportunity to build a new model of collaboration and trust.

The new kind of leadership that you will establish among your top team will have to be cascaded down so you build leadership muscle throughout the organization. Top-down leadership is necessary, but never sufficient. Leaders need to engage "outside the lines" with teams that need to collaborate across the organization. A transformation like the one that lies ahead of you can't be undertaken by the company's top team alone. You need leadership to happen at any level. Given the pace of innovation in a world beyond digital, you need to build that companywide leadership capability that will allow you to move at the speed at which things move in the market.

Don't underestimate the time and effort it takes to engage leaders throughout the organization and build this leadership muscle. Stewart McCrone, Philips's head of Strategy, M&A and Partnerships, admits, "We were a bit naive in how easy and quick it would be to get the next couple of layers of people engaged and on board. We started off in good faith with some good material and some off-sites, but changing a company this size—and even changing twelve hundred leaders—is a much more involved, continuous, complicated, repetitive push than you may think."

If you ask CEOs who transformed their company about their biggest regret, you often hear them talk about not having been decisive enough about repositioning their leadership team. They regret having spent too much time and energy on trying to get one or many team members on board, energy that they ended up not having for other priorities and that often did not even yield the desired outcome.

Your transformation effort won't succeed unless you activate your leadership. Failing to do so—and do so quickly—will be a costly mistake. Succeed, and you will have a powerful and rewarding team that is ready to truly take on the challenging work ahead.

7

Reinvent the Social Contract with Your People

To win in the marketplace you must first win in the workplace.

—Doug Conant, former CEO of the Campbell Soup Company

In the summer of 2020, Cleveland Clinic's CEO Tom Mihaljevic (you met him in chapter 3) established a Chief Caregiver Office. This is how he described its goal to Kelly Hancock, whom he asked to lead it:

> Our vision is really clear. Our organization has a great reputation and a great culture of teamwork. But, I think, we can do much better. We need a unifying role and office to engage the seventy thousand caregivers across our entire health-care system—the nurses, our employed physicians, and our private practice group—to really support the team-of-teams concept. The success of Cleveland Clinic depends not so much on individual contributors but much more on teams of people who each have a critical contribution to make.

"This office," Hancock stresses, "is transformational for us. This is not just another name for the Human Resources department. This office is looking at the value proposition for caregivers, because we know caregivers are our biggest asset in the organization. This is about being the best place to work for caregivers, which is key for Cleveland Clinic being the best place for patients to receive care. And this is about caring for the community by providing education and careers to individuals."

The strategic priorities of the new office may look familiar—supporting health and well-being of caregivers; diversity, equity, and inclusion; caregiver engagement; workforce strategy; talent acquisition—but Cleveland Clinic's take on them and the importance it gives them is different.

"Running a hospital is like flying a spaceship through an asteroid field. Problems come whizzing at you one after another. You have to deal with them now or never—especially those involving patient safety or the quality of care. At Cleveland Clinic, we manage this barrage through a method called tiered huddles," says Mihaljevic.[1] As we discussed in chapter 3, he had established daily tiered huddles when he led Cleveland Clinic Abu Dhabi as a way to have his finger on the pulse of the organization and to engage the whole organization to solve problems as they happen—and extended the practice to the entire network when he became its CEO in 2018. Tiered daily huddles are focused, fifteen-minute conversations that take place every morning among a multidisciplinary team in each unit. They follow a structured format that allows caregivers to speak about the issues of quality, patient safety, experience, and utilization of resources. Caregivers throughout all tier levels resolve issues, often that same day. Issues that can't be resolved by a particular team are escalated to senior teams—tier by tier—within hours. Daily huddles start with the care teams at 7:00 a.m. and escalate to executive leadership, where they conclude, by 11:15 a.m. In this way, not only do the teams communicate with each other to improve how they collaborate, but the whole organization becomes connected and focused on the most important issues that need to be addressed to fulfill its mission.

Mihaljevic explains: "Tiered huddles solve problems in real time. They help us deal with today's problems today, making our organization a better place to be a patient and a better place to work. Tiered huddles are one way we are working to create a culture where every caregiver is capable, empowered, and expected to make improvements every day." Huddles have improved everything from workplace safety to patient experience to quality of care, facility repairs, and staffing. They are, for example, credited for reducing patient falls by 15 percent between January 2017 and August 2019.

Another benefit of the daily huddles is that they have greatly increased the sense of community among caregivers. Hancock remembers how, one day, an issue made its way up through all tiers of the daily huddle to the CEO and the Operations Council, who form tier 6: "On the main campus, we had a pediatric patient who unfortunately was in an end-of-life situation. The family was having a difficult time dealing with the situation and had started to take their emotions out on our caregivers because they weren't able to save their child—going to their homes, threatening them and their families. So, when that was reported out at tier 6, Tom [Mihaljevic] said: 'We have to go up and see that staff. And we have to go see that family. Now.'"

They went up and huddled with the team at the nurses' station— the physicians, nurses, everybody who was involved with that patient. Hancock continues: "Tom said: 'First of all, I want to thank you for the exceptional high-quality empathetic care that you continue to provide to this patient and the family despite the circumstances. I want you to know that we appreciate the professionalism. But I also want you to know that we're going to have a conversation with the family to let them know that there are some boundaries, that they also need to show the respect back in this difficult time.'"

They then went to see the family, listening and empathizing with the family, given the unimaginable pain they were in while also making it clear that that type of behavior and threat to the caregivers was not acceptable. This intervention, while it could not save the life of the patient, had a wonderful impact: everyone was able to support the child, the parents were there, the caregivers were there.

"From a caregiver perspective, to have the CEO of a health system come up to a nursing unit in the children's hospital because they brought something up in a huddle as a concern was powerful," says Hancock. "It builds the community, it shows that we are more than individual contributors, we are a team of teams. The huddles are a tool that allows *all* our people to communicate, *every* day." Daily huddles are also a key tool when the Clinic is rolling out some IT system or new process—they're a great way to communicate with the organization and get immediate feedback on what's working and what is not.

Cleveland Clinic knows that people are its biggest asset. That's why it has created the Chief Caregiver Office, and that's why it goes out of its way to create a sense of community and belonging among its people. That's also why it has established this powerful way of communicating across the entire organization, every day, so people can raise issues and contribute solutions to make the Clinic a better place to receive and give care.

As we argued in chapter 2, the nature of value creation in the beyond digital world requires differentiating capabilities that are complex and expensive—and that depend on people to build and deliver them. No matter how many investments you may make in new technologies and businesses, if you can't get your people to embrace them and build them into your differentiated capabilities, your investments risk being wasted. (See "The Importance of the New Model of People Engagement in the Beyond Digital World.") Indeed, almost every leader we interviewed in the course of our research said they not only learned that they needed to engage with their people to

The Importance of the New Model of People Engagement in the Beyond Digital World

Companies have long talked about the importance of engaging their people, yet employees remain largely disconnected from the purpose of most organizations. The incentives have shifted meaningfully, though, because the nature of value and competitive advantage, and thus the nature of work, have changed. Today's value-creation model inherently relies on integrating people—their experiences, skills, judgment, and values—with technology, assets, and processes to create the differentiated capabilities that are at the heart of companies' ability to compete.

Differentiation in this model cannot solely rely on, for example, smart technology—all the smartest technology in the world can be beaten by the next innovation, or even a simple reimagination of how to use existing technology. Even in areas where forecasts indicate that technology and robots are likely to replace humans (for example, warehouse management or discrete manufacturing), people remain essential to learn how to work with the new technologies and create value from them. Companies also cannot rely on just being smarter than everyone else because of, for example, a really clever founder or a well-recognized leadership team. That might help with some thinking at the top of the organization, but getting anything done with customers on the front lines or anywhere else in the organization still relies on harnessing the capabilities of a large group of people and helping them succeed.

Every single reimagined place we've talked about in this book needed significant work from an entire organization to drive the type of change required. Building a system of privileged insights,

(continued)

for instance, will take leaders across many functions to rethink how the company interacts with customers and uses the insights. Engaging an ecosystem will take dozens, and likely hundreds or in some cases thousands, of your employees to learn new ways of working on the outside—looking out for the interests of customers, your ecosystem partners, and your organization all at the same time. A way of competing based on differentiated capabilities requires teams to deliver clear outcomes—and needs a workforce that arrives every day motivated to solve the challenges and opportunities ahead. It needs a team of people who can do more diverse, continually evolving, and increasingly cross-functional work while also constantly improving what they do and how they do it. It needs a workforce that is fully in the game because solving a much larger customer or societal challenge won't be easy.

The scale of this transformation requires a new social contract that supports a fundamentally more engaged and committed team that will shape and secure your place in the world. The challenge is that most companies struggle to create the kind of citizen-led ownership that is needed. Our research shows that in most organizations, the majority of employees—the individuals responsible for executing your strategic vision—don't understand the goals of the organization, what the company is trying to uniquely accomplish, and how their jobs fit into the broader vision. In a recent worldwide survey of employees across industries conducted by Strategy&, only 28 percent of respondents reported feeling fully connected to their company's purpose. Just 39 percent said they could clearly see the value they create; a mere 22 percent agreed that their jobs allowed them to fully leverage their strengths; and only 34 percent thought they strongly contribute to their company's success. More than half said they weren't even "somewhat motivated"—or "somewhat passionate" or "somewhat excited"—about their jobs.[a]

Think about it. Only a third of employees feel they truly understand what the company is trying to do, are engaged with the work, or feel that they are really contributing. That means two-thirds are not engaged—they are either not rowing or are rowing in a direction other than the one you've chosen. So much for your grand strategic vision—without having the team deeply engaged with you, that vision will likely remain just a dream.

But here's the good news. Our research also confirms that employees who understand and embrace their organization's purpose are more motivated and enthusiastic about their jobs than employees who don't experience a sense of purpose. Indeed, the Strategy& survey found that 63 percent of employees in companies that have clearly defined and communicated how they create value for customers say they're motivated, versus 31 percent at other companies; and 65 percent say they're passionate about their work, versus 32 percent in other companies.

Today companies need a more holistic, collaborative way of engaging that connects people's intrinsic values and motivations to the values and purpose of the company. It requires shifting the leadership model from making sure people understand what to do and how to do it, to empowering them to do what is needed.

This means that, as a leader, you will need to make connecting with, listening to, and understanding your people a more significant priority than it may have been in the past. You will need to understand their motivations and help them connect to your company's purpose. You will need to learn what they need so they can successfully deliver the value propositions you aim for. You will need to

(continued)

empower them to shape the ways of working your organization needs. You will need to help them collaborate and solve problems on the spot in a way that is consistent with your company's values. You will need your people to pull you forward, instead of being pulled along by you.

In the past, engaging people was typically approached as an HR or morale problem. To succeed in today's environment, however, creating engagement will need to be a central pillar of your leader-ship agenda.

a. Strategy&, "Our Research on the Connection between Strategic Purpose and Motivation," https://www.strategyand.pwc.com/gx/en/unique-solutions/capabilities -driven-strategy/approach/research-motivation.html.

succeed with their transformation but wished they had done so much earlier in their journey.

So, how do you get your people to take ownership? How do you get people to embrace change? How do you get people to not rest on their laurels? How do you help them volunteer ideas and take the right risks? Like Cleveland Clinic, you will need to connect people directly with your company's purpose and value-creation system. You will need to give people the means to succeed. You will need to give them mechanisms to raise issues and contribute solutions. And, like Cleveland Clinic, you will need to do all of this not on an exception basis, or a once-a-year change effort, but as part of your daily work. In other words, you will need to invert the traditional employer-employee relationship to reinvent your company's social contract with your people—putting them at the center of how you create value and at the top of your leadership team's priorities.

Reinventing the Social Contract with Your People

To get people fully engaged, you will need to fundamentally rethink the "contract" you have with them, so they bring their best to work every day *and* contribute to the company's mission. We don't mean the legal document that states the terms of employment, but the implicit contract between the company and its people that makes sure that both parties get what they need to thrive. In the past, this contract focused on compensation and benefits and was rather unilateral. Employees were asked to perform a set of activities for which the company would pay them, and that's where the responsibility often ended. That contract now covers many dimensions in addition to compensation and benefits. In the past, companies thought about what they needed to offer to attract employees. Now, the perspective is changing: companies listen to employees and prospects and try to provide an environment so they opt in. This winds up being particularly true in a constrained job market—but the job market is always constrained when you are looking for specialists and those who are willing to go above and beyond in service of your place in the world. It's not that compensation is not an important factor—and for some that may be all that is desired/required—but increasingly leaders must broaden their thinking about what motivates people in their jobs.

The successful companies we've studied rethink the following six dimensions of their contract with people to turn it into a powerful system of engagement:

- **Purpose.** They make their company worthy of their people's engagement by articulating their purpose in a way that is meaningful.

- **Contribution.** They give people the opportunity to be part of the solution, to innovate and contribute.

- **Community.** They involve people in shaping the company's culture and connect them together in supportive teams so they can develop something great together.

- **Development.** They help people acquire the skills and experiences that are required to thrive in the beyond digital age.

- **Means.** They give people the time and resources to build and scale the differentiating capabilities they have committed to.

- **Rewards.** They recognize that the way people perceive value goes beyond compensation and offer a more comprehensive system of rewards.

Purpose: Be Worthy of Your People's Engagement

To go beyond digital, you must articulate your company's purpose in a way that makes your institution worthy of your people's engagement and that makes them want to contribute their energies. To do so, you will need to see how their personal sense of purpose connects with your company's, so they choose to align themselves with your organization.

Over the past decade, "purpose" has become a management buzzword. Since 2010, it has appeared in the titles of more than four hundred business and leadership books and thousands of articles. No wonder: people want their lives to have meaning, and, given how much time is spent at work, large groups of individuals—not just millennials—want to work for organizations whose missions and business philosophies resonate with them intellectually and emotionally.

However, what we mean by *purpose* goes well beyond a lofty statement. You must clearly articulate your company's place in the world in a way that explains the value you bring to customers and society and that motivates your people. In fact, it is through this articulation of what the company does better than anyone else that you find direct connection to your teams. Human beings struggle to relate to products. Yes, a few brilliant designers or engineers may feel a great connection, but most of your employees will not be associated directly with the individual products or services that your company offers and will better understand how they fit in when you are clear about how your differentiated capabilities come to life. That way, they can explain what role they play and come to work every day engaged and energized to deliver.

When people understand and embrace your organization's purpose, they're inspired not only to come to work but also to go the extra mile. Philips's Stewart McCrone explains: "One of the good things about moving into health technology is that it is an extremely attractive space for people—and millennials, in particular—to be involved with. Saving people's lives is something we do en masse, every day—and something people want to be involved with. Eighty percent of the people who apply for a job at Philips mention our purpose of improving 2.5 billion lives by 2030 as one of the reasons why they want to join us. It is really inspirational for new joiners but also those of us who have been around longer."

As you map out your transformation journey, use this watershed moment to assess how your purpose can speak to your people, your ecosystems, and your other stakeholders. What is meaningful to your people and to your customers? What difference do your company's products and services make in society? Use those insights to help shape how you connect your company's purpose to your people's motivations. For example, as we noted in chapter 3, the impetus for Komatsu's transformation was to address the serious labor shortages in Japan's construction industry by providing advanced machinery and software solutions that digitize construction sites and enable customers to work more precisely and efficiently while using much less human labor than in the past. Says Chikashi Shike, who heads Komatsu's Smart Construction Promotion Division, "When a project provides social value above and beyond what benefits the customer, it's not hard to get people on board."

Eli Lilly is interesting in how it made its case on both logical and emotional grounds. It had a simple and logical rationale for the Years YZ transformation we described in chapter 6: four of the company's most important drugs, which together made up about 40 percent of its revenues, were coming off patent around the same time, threatening the company's continued existence as an independent entity. If Lilly was to survive, it had to double down on innovation, modernizing its R&D program and replenishing the product pipeline. But the company did not stop at these logical arguments. It added an emotional punch: it reaffirmed its historical purpose of discovering and developing pharmaceuticals that improve peoples' lives, as well as its commitment to the economic well-being of the communities of Indianapolis and central Indiana, where Lilly is based. In his communication to employees, CEO John Lechleiter did not focus on what the transformation program meant for Lilly but on what it meant for patients, reminding everyone that patients need Lilly's help.

And while people are generally inspired by organizations that take on society's biggest challenges, most employees look for clarity in how the company creates value and how they can contribute to it. Most importantly, you must live your purpose. Day in and day out, you have to demonstrate behaviors and make choices consistent with your purpose to earn your people's engagement.

Contribution: Make People Part of the Solution

Our research found that successful companies engaged people deep within their organization and across their ecosystem early in their transformations. The earlier you engage your people to shape the change, the easier it is to enable difficult changes to happen—including those that may have very personal impacts and consequences for employees, such as meaningful changes to people's roles and teams, such as integration of new technologies, and obviously such as impacts to their employment. Without this engagement, companies learned the hard way that people can't seem to get over their fear of technology, struggle to understand why they should change what seemed to be working well, and even insist that leadership has it all wrong and is actually harming the company. If people feel that change is imposed on them and that they had no voice in the process, they often think the change won't work and resist it.

We're not arguing that all change must be consensus-driven. In fact, many of your hardest decisions will not be. But there is no way around creating venues to bring your teams along and have them contribute.

Engage your people to shape the change. Once you've articulated your purpose, you'll need to build in structures to get feedback from your teams and allow your people to define how they take the journey to achieve your specific goals. People can see how they fit in and decide how they can contribute.

Cleveland Clinic's daily tiered huddles are a powerful way to get people across the organization to raise issues and contribute solutions. Some companies add a formal, often annual, type of innovation challenge to the mix. At Microsoft, the annual growth hack has become a tradition. As CEO Satya Nadella writes,

> Every year, employees—engineers, marketers, all professions—prepare in their home countries for the OneWeek growth hack like students preparing for a science fair, working in teams to hack problems they feel passionate about and then developing presentations designed to win votes from their colleagues. Gathered in tents named Hacknado and Codapalooza, they consume thousands of pounds of doughnuts, chicken, baby carrots, energy bars, coffee, and the

occasional beer to fuel their creativity. Programmers and analysts suddenly transform into carnival barkers, selling their ideas to anyone willing to listen. Reactions range from polite questions to vigorous debate and challenges. In the end, votes sent from smartphones are tallied, projects evaluated, winners celebrated. A few projects even receive funding as new business efforts.[2]

Titan taps into the creativity of its employees to come up with big ideas for future growth—while being very clear about what it takes for ideas to be a fit with the company's identity. Former CEO Bhaskar Bhat explains:

> We launched a program called Ignitor, where we encouraged teams to come up with ideas for the future. And we published what we called Titan's Hexagon. There are six elements that ought to be considered for selecting a business to pursue. It must be an unorganized, not regulated, category; it must be a personal product; the category must be amenable to branding; design should be an important element in the purchase consideration; cost should not be an important driver; and the category should not be intensively competitive. We will never enter the mobile phone business, for example. When we launched the Ignitor program, we had seven hundred entries. We went through a jury process, and out of a final short list of fourteen, Taneira, the ethnic wear brand for women, emerged.

Engaging your employees can—and should—happen in a multitude of ways. Your goal is to not only include them in the process but to wire into your capabilities system the collective ideas of people that are close to your customers and empower them to execute the changes you put in place to shape your future.

Engage your ecosystem. Getting employees within the four walls of your company to contribute isn't enough. Since the success of the transformation you're embarking on depends not just on your own organization but on many different stakeholders, such as suppliers, partners, shareholders, and customers, you need to engage your larger ecosystems. Organizations increasingly rely on key partners for critical differentiating capabilities and talent, and these partners need to be engaged in your vision. For example, creative marketing experts, although often outside the organization's boundaries, are frequently intimately engaged in both the articulation and the execution of the company's vision and purpose.

As discussed in chapter 5, Microsoft's adoption of its AI/cloud first strategy required transformation of its commercial sales organization and practices. Since Microsoft relied on its vast partner network to go to market—IT companies, such as software companies or systems integrators, but also telecommunication companies or conventional manufacturers and retailers that built solutions based on Microsoft technologies—the role of these partners also needed to change significantly. Like Microsoft itself, partner companies needed to focus more on cloud services than on-premises infrastructure services and more on user experiences, regardless of the device being used, rather than solely on desktop experiences.

Microsoft invested in partner training and developed sales tools to help partners adapt. But it didn't just train its partners to change; it changed, too. Nicola Hodson, vice president of Field Transformation in Global Sales, Marketing and Operations, remembers how Microsoft shifted away from just giving partners tools: "We used to build a lot of tools for our sellers and then tell everyone to use them. But, guess what? . . . nobody really liked them, and nobody bothered to use them. We were basically spending a lot of money and not getting a whole heap of success." Instead, Microsoft promised to develop the tools partners needed to do the job—if those partners jumped in and helped.

Microsoft now has two global sessions a month with the development team to gather and prioritize ideas. Says Hodson, "The road map is jointly developed. The feedback is jointly heard. The road map is very iterative. We made something that was static, one-way, and not fit-for-purpose into something that is massively dynamic, two-way, and really starting to hit the spot for people."

Community: Connect People in Supportive Teams So They Can Develop Something Great Together

For employees to step up and help you drive the required transformation, you need to give them opportunities to connect in teams where they can safely express themselves and work together with people they care about toward accomplishing something that matters. You will want to create situations where people feel that doing their job makes a difference and contributes to others on the team. You will want people to feel like they can fully be themselves and be supported in an inclusive team. That's when you get powerful teams and organizations that are willing to stop doing what they did in the past and try something new.

This sense of community is a key component of the contract between the company and its people. You will need to help your people feel safe to express themselves with honesty and to care enough about each other to say and do what is needed to create the value your company is out to deliver. Feeling that "I want to be here, I want to work with these individuals, I feel comfortable in this environment" is crucial. This isn't just about everybody being happy. It is about being happy in a model that is productive for the company and for what it is trying to achieve. The year spent working from home because of the Covid-19 pandemic has challenged efforts to build community, and special attention will need to be paid to innovate new ways of building community as companies implement new models for work with increased remote working.

Some companies still bet on instilling competition between employees, making them believe that they will succeed only if they're better than their colleagues. In a recent survey we ran on the topic of teaming and collaboration, only 34 percent of respondents indicated that their relationship with their day-to-day team members wasn't competitive. That model of internal competition, however, isn't working in a world where value creation relies on bringing people with different skills together to build greatness, rather than hoping for innovation from motivated individuals focused on outperforming their peers. Fifty-seven percent of our survey takers said they thought that internal competition leads to negative outcomes such as bad teaming and less risk taking.

This sense of community is, of course, tied to your company's culture. Your people will ask questions such as: "Do I share the company's values—and do my coworkers share them?" "Are the behaviors we are asked to exhibit in line with my values?"

Philips's Carla Kriwet spent a lot of time on engaging her team around the company's cultural values:

> I think it's very important to make these values relevant for people. If you just tell them, "We have these five cultural values," they look at them and say, "Yeah. Makes sense." You will only drive it home if you really engage people around the values, if you say, "Okay, Quality First—how does that fit with us missing the mark in the market on quality? What is the leadership issue that prevents our people from speaking up if there are quality issues? Are we empowering them well enough? Let's have a discussion about that." You need to trigger people to really think about their role in it: "What are you actually doing? What is your role? What does it mean for you? Where are you struggling with this? If you're struggling, how are you bringing it up?" These kinds of discussions are more important than saying, "You promised to deliver twenty

systems and now it's only eighteen. What about the two?" That's water under the bridge if you don't change the under- lying behaviors.

Development: Make It a Priority to Invest in Helping People Develop the Skills and Experiences They Need

You will be asking people to work in new ways—acquiring different skills, using new technologies, working on unfamiliar and more fluid teams alongside new partners and platforms. Some of the changes you will need to make—such as asking someone to work outside the organizational boundaries in which they've spent their careers or to write code for a robot that might take over their job—can be uncomfortable. Helping people develop the skills they need to thrive in this new environment is key if you want them to fully engage. It is also an obvious business necessity: 72 percent of CEOs taking part in the PwC 24th Annual Global CEO Survey (conducted in early 2021) said they were concerned about the lack of key skills.[3] To succeed in the beyond digital world, you will need to make training and upskilling a strategic priority.

Your people will need to not only know how to use technology but feel safe doing so in the midst of constant technology changes that threaten to dislocate their jobs. Every company, therefore, needs to have some strategy to help people develop the requisite technology skills and agility that your capabilities system will undoubtedly require.

As part of its commercial transformation program, for example, Microsoft ran an extensive upskilling program. Nicola Hodson remembers, "It was obvious that the skills needed to help our customers with those much deeper and bigger digital transformations were different from what we had. We needed our people to have conversations with C-level customers, talk about the deep business challenges that the customer might be facing and the pace of change, and be able to understand what Microsoft can bring to the party in order to help that customer with those deeper business challenges. That's very different from selling software or services, which we'd typically previously done at lower level in the organization with the CIO's team." Microsoft retrained everyone in the organization on the challenge of selling and started to do a lot of work on deep industry training.

Not just salespeople needed upskilling. It became clear that customers were actually demanding that everyone in the organization become more technical. Jean-Philippe Courtois recounts, "Technical certification is now mandatory for all of our people. Each and every one of us is going through some massive technical certification forums, different levels depending on your role. Over a six-month period, it will typically add up to 100 to 150 hours of online training. The more technical your job, the higher the bar. And by the way, we're doing the same with our partners and customers—massive upskilling investment to become digital." To make the training program more engaging and easier to consume, Microsoft puts a lot of attention into gamifying the learning and making it more snackable, aiming for people to seek out the training rather than being force-fed.

Microsoft has also launched a coaching initiative to complement the formal teaching. As Courtois recounts, "We've been partnering with a company to help our managers shift away from the traditional command-and-control model that you find in most large organizations and become what you call 'coaching managers.' Instead of telling people, 'Here's what you need to do in your job, here are the reds, the greens, and the yellows of the scorecard, and this is the way to do it; go and get the job done,' we want our managers to have a more open dialogue and ask a few insightful questions to figure out, one by one, the best way to get to the customer success."

Sometimes, simply stating the newly desired skills will surface people you did not know of, who have those skills and who are energized by your vision. As Honeywell was setting up its new Connected Aircraft business (see chapter 5), for example, the leader anticipated that the new organization would need to recruit from outside the company for engineering, data analytics, and other skills. But it turned out that many employees, who had been jaded for years and or had stopped offering ideas because they did not go anywhere, stepped up and wanted to be part of the team. They wound up with a 60/40 mix of internal versus external hires, contrary to their initial assumption.

For people who have skills or are in roles that will become less critical, you need to help them understand how they will need to change or how they can update their skills. This will require patience. Many employees will require in-depth training in new skills, processes, and capabilities, and you will need to give them time and budget to invest in their development. Companies often use a mix of in-house development, executive education, and external certification programs. We now also see leading companies starting to set up development programs together with their ecosystem partners, thereby accomplishing two goals at once.

As you're making these investments, keep your broader purpose in mind. You want your whole ecosystem to work together better and your people to be more productive and fulfilled. You also want to acknowledge and support your employees' needs and desires for workplace diversity and equality, more flexible working conditions, and more meaning and community.

Means: Invest in Building Differentiating Capabilities So People Have the Opportunity to Deliver on the Purpose

Even though you have articulated your purpose clearly and communicated it effectively, employees will be unable to fully engage if you don't invest in the design, scaling, and implementation of the differentiating capabilities that you have identified as critical. Nothing is more demotivating for employees than working in an area that's been identified as critical but that's not being resourced adequately.

This issue will require particular attention when business conditions are difficult. You will need to ensure that the impetus for cost management and efficiency doesn't cut off the capability building that will enable you to create advantage in the future. At Lilly, all through the painful cost-cutting that the YZ transformation required—as the company took out $1 billion in costs, laid off thousands of employees, and faced Wall Street pressure for further austerity—the leadership team increased investment into R&D each year. Between 2007 and 2016, R&D as percentage of sales increased from 19 percent to 25 percent.[4]

Where will you find the resources required to build the capabilities that are at the heart of your success? How will you be able to fund relevant ideas your people will come up with? Since you will need to outspend your competitors in those areas, you will need to reduce spending to a minimum on everything else. You will need to treat every cost as an investment, understanding that the same amount of money could be used to either enable your people to develop amazingly powerful distinctive capabilities, or fund incoherent activities that will end up holding your company back.

Managing costs in this way moves you to a new level of financial discipline. When times are good, you don't dilute your investment dollars by making bets on dozens of new projects. Instead, you figure out the areas where you are most likely to succeed and focus your investments there. When times are tough, you don't cut costs across the board. Instead, you find ways to double down on your strategic priorities and cut everything else.

More than money is needed, though. You also need to put in place the structures, systems, processes, and controls that enable employees to deliver on the organization's vison and purpose. Left unchecked, misalignment spawns toxicity and cynicism and kills the engagement that you need to win.

Last but not least, you need to explicitly give people the bandwidth to spend meaningful amounts of time on projects that may not be directly related to their current jobs but that might lead to future innovations or better ways to execute. The most famous example is "20 percent time" at Google, where the company's founders have, since 2004, encouraged employees to spend one day per week on a project of their own choosing or creation that could pay off for the company in the future. While this might seem like a luxury or an inefficiency to leaders with more traditional corporate backgrounds, and requires both higher staffing levels and different cultural norms, the payoff from empowering people to work "on the future" can have huge payoffs: At Google, both Gmail and Google Maps started as "20 percent time" projects.

Rewards: Compensation Is Important, but It's Not Everything

Monetary compensation is important, both in recruiting the right talent and in designing an equitable mechanism to share the company's profits. But regardless of how important a paycheck is to any individual, the point of the social contract is to recognize that nearly all employees value other forms of rewards, too. They like seeing that they have contributed meaningfully to some aspect of your transformation, that they have been a key part of a customer's positive experience, or that they helped to assemble one of your outcome-oriented teams. Individuals also appreciate being recognized for what they do—even something as simple as "employee of the month" makes people feel valued, and the beyond digital world provides loads of opportunities to recognize individuals and teams in creative, new ways.

Saleh Mosaibah, former CEO of STC Pay, summarizes it well:

Employees need trust and support. Yes, they need to be compensated well, but there are many soft things that they value more than money. And if you pay them more but you don't give them that respect they need, and you don't give them the freedom they want, and you don't make them part of the decisions, they will leave and go somewhere else. Some of our employees are getting offers of double their salaries, but they're not interested in leaving. They just believe in STC Pay. They believe that their future is here. They believe that they're making a serious impact on society. They're so passionate, and they want to be part of the success story.

While you won't win the race for talent only through compensation and benefits, it will become increasingly important for you to tightly link individual and team incentives to the impact people have on the realization of the company's strategy and purpose. You need to be clear where the company's new pools of value are and how you measure success around them. Then link people's incentives to the fulfillment of those measures. Whether the reward is going to be equity, cash, or other forms of benefits depends, among other things, on the time horizon over which the person's contribution is going to pay off, for how long you wish to retain them, and what motivates that individual. Managing a team of people with very different compensation formulas will certainly add to the complexity—but it is what is typically needed in this more complicated world.

. . .

One story that highlights several of these areas is what STC Pay does to engage its employees to continuously push the limits of what's possible (see chapter 4 for more on how STC Pay built a system of privileged insights with its customers). Former CEO Saleh Mosaibah is against having an innovation center. "Innovation is a principle, like collaboration. Innovation and collaboration have to be done by everyone. You don't create a collaboration team—and in the same spirit, I don't think you should create an innovation department," he says. "I've seen many innovation departments in large companies. They're often quite theoretical and far from reality. The real innovation, however, comes from those people who are on the ground, either from people who are seeing customers every day and selling services, or from those who are building the technology and developing the software and who see how it's being used by customers. Those usually are the main innovators."

For Mosaibah, success goes back to personal commitment of employees: "Are you really hooked to STC Pay and do you think that your future is with STC Pay for the next five years? The minute this is sealed, people will care about the company's future. They will see themselves as executives, as managers, as directors, as part of the company in the coming five years. They will not just worry about hitting this year's KPIs, but they will have that longer-term view and they will come up with ideas that may only pay off in two years' time."

Mosaibah also believes in putting the right healthy pressure on people, in giving them stretch targets and tight resources, because there will be no way but innovating. "Pressure is always healthy, as long as it's not a mental pressure. As long as it comes with trust, with freedom, and with support. When that's the case, people usually innovate; they work harder, they are more dedicated, and they come up with more innovations."

Trust, freedom and support are key. "People need to see that they're part of the decisions, that they can change directions," Mosaibah says. He often got calls from employees questioning some of his decisions, and many times he agreed with them and looked into the matter again, changing direction if needed. "We don't have this culture of people blindly following what the CEO says. All executives are approachable, not because we're humble or we're good humans, but because it makes good business sense and it is their right as employees. They know the business—in many cases better than us. It's the right thing for our business that we keep listening to employees who are facing customers every day and who might have very valuable feedback that can change the whole company's direction."

. . .

You have a difficult and complex task ahead. But with engaged employees and ecosystem partners on your side, you've got an incredible source of strength for change. Not only will these individuals be motivated to deliver the value proposition you promise, but they will also hold you accountable to deliver on the transformation.

8

Disrupt Your Own Leadership Approach

To be aware of a single shortcoming in oneself is more useful than to be aware of a thousand in someone else.

—Tenzin Gyatso, the 14th and current Dalai Lama

One of the things that struck us when we conducted the research for this book is how consistently the leaders we interviewed emphasized that they themselves had to transform at least as much as their companies did. Without disrupting their own leadership approach, they wouldn't have been able to reimagine how their company creates value, to re-architect their organization and leadership team, or to engage their people in meaningful ways. In other words, without disrupting their own leadership approach, they would not have been able to transform their companies and position them for success in the beyond digital age.

Philips's CEO Frans van Houten recalls, "The leadership journey that was required for me was a profound one." Van Houten joined

Philips in 1986, starting in marketing and sales, and has held multiple global leadership positions across the company on three continents. He considers himself lucky to have had the chance to lead large organizations since the early 2000s. An important step on his leadership journey was taking on the responsibility for the Asia-Pacific region of the consumer electronics business in 1999. "Cor Boonstra [former CEO of Philips] sent me there to learn to lead people rather than just being the smart-ass in the class. That was an important confrontation for me that I will never forget," he says.

In 2004, van Houten became the CEO of the semiconductor business and led its 2006 spin-off into NXP Semiconductors, where he stayed on as CEO. As he describes it, "That was again a big leadership transformation for me. We had very demanding owners, and I was not a semiconductor expert. That meant I had to drive change without letting myself be held back by people who knew much more about semiconductors but resisted change. I did a lot of transformative change during those years. It worked pretty well, even though eventually I was asked to go in the depth of the crisis, at the end of 2008. It was a humbling experience—and that is probably also good. But I knew that if one door closes, other ones open." Eighteen months later, he returned to Philips as COO and CEO heir apparent.

Van Houten reflects on his transformation experience:

> Throughout those years, I became more and more aware that you need to reach results through people and that understanding and influencing their beliefs and behaviors is essential in order to achieve results. It's also the time when I took a bigger interest in better understanding my own motives, why I do things. I am very interested in the deeper motives of how people are wired and how their belief system influences their behaviors. And I've brought those softer sides of management into my roles and exposed our larger groups of people to these insights.

Another aspect I also came to appreciate more and more is that leaders need to be authentic. You cannot talk nonsense to a large part of the organization. In order to have the strength and the energy to lead a large organization for multiple years, you've got to be in your own strength, and therefore you've got to be authentic. And if you can marry that with purpose, that gives you a very powerful recipe: people see you being authentic for a larger purpose, not for your own benefit. And that leads to followership, especially if you can do it with enough room for other people to also become successful.

We've heard similar stories from many other leaders: stories where leaders stretched outside their comfort zone to acquire knowledge, stories where they deliberately took on roles to gain experiences that would help position them for success, stories where they discovered strengths as well as stories of how they discovered that some habits that had served them well had to be cast aside as the world moves beyond digital. Through their Citi Holdings experience, Jane Fraser, current CEO of Citigroup, and Michael Corbat, her predecessor, gained deep insights into the inner workings of the company—almost like taking it apart and putting it back together—and they learned a lot about the consequences of good and bad decisions as well as the risk and people challenges. Tom Mihaljevic, MD, CEO and President of Cleveland Clinic, can draw on his unique experience setting up the hospital in Abu Dhabi from a clean sheet and use it to improve clinical operations in Cleveland and locations where the health care system is expanding. Hiroaki Nakanishi could build on his experience gained while turning around Hitachi Global Storage Technologies (HGST) to objectively assess the challenges the parent company was facing.

Frans van Houten, Jane Fraser, Michael Corbat, Tom Mihaljevic, Hiroaki Nakanishi, and other leaders like them had to develop themselves so they were ready to lead their companies through the transformations that are required. This journey isn't easy for the companies—and it isn't easy for their leaders. In fact, the journeys the companies we researched had to go through and the ones their leaders needed to undertake had many similarities. Leaders also need to reimagine their place and purpose in the world. They need to identify the few core leadership skills that are essential for them. They then need to look in the mirror and determine what they're missing. And they need to work out how they're going to fill the gaps between where they are and where they need to be. Like companies, leaders don't need to develop all those capabilities on their own. Companies can partner with other players in their ecosystem to deliver value to customers, and leaders are part of a team where members can balance each other's weaknesses.

The Characteristics of Successful Leaders in the Digital Age

Despite the uniqueness of each journey, we have observed a common set of characteristics among the leaders who transformed their companies, both in our ongoing work with leaders as well as our research for this book. We have found no single attribute that makes CEOs successful, but instead a collection of necessary qualities, many of which actually at first look somewhat contradictory. In *Strategy That Works*, for example, we have discussed extensively the need for leaders to balance deep strategic insight with strong execution skills, which goes against the traditional view that leaders should either be great visionaries or great operators.[1] Our colleague Blair Sheppard published six such paradoxes in his book *Ten Years to Midnight*.[2] We found the paradoxes highly relevant and helpful in our own research with the companies for this book. (See "The Six Leadership Paradoxes.")

The Six Leadership Paradoxes

In his recent book *Ten Years to Midnight*, Blair Sheppard and his team sum up the concerns that people all over the world have in what he calls the ADAPT framework:[a]

- *A*symmetry of wealth and opportunity

- *D*isruption wrought by the unexpected and often problematic consequences of technology and climate

- *A*ge disparities—stresses caused by very young or very old populations

- *P*olarization leading to the breakdown in global and national consensus

- Loss of *T*rust in the institutions that underpin and stabilize society

The team studied leaders who took the time to understand the origin and threats of the crises that result from these concerns and who "provided creative solutions when others were still struggling with identifying the problems." They found that those leaders reconciled (and used to their advantage) distinctive characteristics that on the surface seem quite odd: six leadership paradoxes.

Sheppard writes, "At the heart of each paradox is a core tension that involves contradictory-yet-interrelated elements that exist simultaneously and persist over time. When these characteristics are out of sync, the outcome is almost always disappointing. Think of the high-profile executive hero who saves an organization from the brink of disaster but lacks the humility to seek advice or the ability to change course; more than likely, that campaign will end in failure."

(continued)

Six paradoxes of leadership

Strategic executor
How do you execute effectively while also being highly strategic?

Strategic: To find insights and observations by looking to the future to inform decision-making today.
Executor: To deliver exquisitely on today's challenges.

High-integrity politician
How do you navigate the politics of getting things to happen and retain your character?

High-integrity: To maintain integrity and build trust in all interactions.
Politician: To accrue support, negotiate, form coalitions, overcome resistance to maintain progress.

Traditioned innovator
How do you use the past to help direct your future success while also creating a culture that allows innovation, failure, learning, and growth?

Traditioned: To connect deeply with the purpose of the original idea, and bring this value to the present day.
Innovator: To drive innovation and try new things; have the courage to fail and allow others to do so.

Tech-savvy humanist
How do you become increasingly tech savvy and remember that organizations are run by people, for people?

Tech-savvy: To drive technology enhancement that generates future success.
Humanist: To deeply understand human effectiveness in any given system.

Humble hero
How do you have the confidence to act in an uncertain world and the humility to recognize when you are wrong?

Humble: To foster deep personal resilience in self and others, recognizing when to help and be helped.
Hero: To exude confidence, with competitive flair and gravitas.

Globally minded localist
How do you navigate a world that is increasingly both global and local?

Globally minded: To be agnostic about belief system and market structure and be a student of the world.
Localist: To be fully committed to the success of a local market.

Source: Based on Blair H. Sheppard, *Ten Years to Midnight: Four Urgent Global Crises and Their Strategic Solutions* (San Francisco: Berrett-Koehler Publishers, 2020).

Inhabiting both elements of a paradox, Sheppard continues, "is not an easy undertaking. Many leaders—indeed, all of us—gravitate toward our sweet spots; to what we do well. But, by definition, leadership paradoxes require that we use our best skills while also improving those traits we would prefer to avoid."

a. Blair H. Sheppard, *Ten Years to Midnight: Four Urgent Global Crises and Their Strategic Solutions* (San Francisco: Berrett-Koehler Publishers, 2020), 162.

Every leader will bring their own strengths to the job—and much like organizations should find and leverage their hidden powers, so should you. You've been given the opportunity to lead your organization for a reason, so make sure you emphasize your strengths, particularly as they can be used to drive the transformation forward. But you also need to recognize that today's environment demands a broader leadership approach. You can use these paradoxes as a map that will guide you in your own development. You won't necessarily need to become master at all six paradoxes, but at a minimum you will need to develop a deep sensitivity for the paradoxes that allows you to spot when you or your team aren't getting the balance right. The paradoxes will help you recognize your own gaps and focus your energy on what matters most. They will help you determine what skills you will want to develop and where you will partner with others who are masters.

Strategic Executor

While we've covered at length all the ways that leaders need to be great strategists these days, being a good strategist isn't enough. Leaders need to be equally skilled at execution. They need to have their heads in the sky and their feet in the mud. They need to know what the company is capable of executing before deciding on the destination and engaging on the journey. And they need to be deeply involved in the execution—be it in the design of the organization, key systems or career models, or the execution of upskilling efforts or customer experience design sessions. They need to make sure that execution matches strategic intent while signaling to the organization that they won't stop anywhere short of excellence in the areas that are key to success.

Howard Schultz's return to Starbucks as CEO in 2008 shows what a strategic executor looks like. Based on his original vision of a "third place," beyond office and home, Schultz drove all the way down into the details—ending the use of flavor-locked bags of beans, so coffee aromas would again fill the stores as baristas scooped beans out of bins and ground them; moving big espresso machines so customers could again see the baristas making drinks; removing products from around the cash register that, while generating revenue, detracted from what he saw as the experience that distinguished Starbucks from competitors such as McDonald's and Dunkin' Donuts.

Two leaders from our research who exemplify this strategic executor characteristic are Tim Mahoney, former president and CEO of Honeywell Aerospace, and Carl Esposito, then president of Electronic Solutions (you met them in chapter 5). Back in the 1990s, they'd already started developing a vision about how connectivity could revolutionize aviation—long before the necessary technology was available—and they were ready when it was. Carl Esposito recalls, "There were a few of us who had that broader vision of where we needed to go, and we could see how the pieces that we were putting together were the elements of the broader strategy: the acquisition, the connectivity pipes, the digitization of the avionics and electronics and the mechanical systems."

When the time was ripe to start making the connectivity strategy a reality, they did not delegate execution. They got their hands dirty, worrying even about details like posting jobs for product managers and changing reporting lines of operations people in their HR systems. A lot of detailed work was needed, and they stayed very much involved. Esposito remembers, "We had to find people on the connectivity and the services side that had a much more digital bent to them. We had to think about how our business systems had to transform from legacy into more service offerings. We had to understand how to price and value those new kinds of capabilities that we could offer and what the business models were behind that."

Esposito also played a key role in bringing together people from lots of different product areas and expertise to think about what would happen if they connected individual aircraft components—engines, weather radars, and so on—to the internet or got them to share data in new ways. They went product line by product line and developed business cases, customer care-abouts, and value propositions.

Tim Mahoney and Carl Esposito aren't just visionaries or just operators. They are true strategic executors, and the world beyond digital needs more of them.

Tech-Savvy Humanist

Leaders in today's world need to understand and use technology to drive success. In the past, leaders may have gotten away with delegating the company's technology challenges to their chief information officer or chief digital officer, but that approach doesn't work anymore. Now that technology is a key enabler for almost everything a company does—innovation, operations, supply chain management, sales and marketing, finance, HR, or any other area—every leader needs to understand what technology can do for the company. This is key not only when reimagining the company's place in the world but also when redefining how work gets done, how the company's differentiating capabilities are going to be scaled up across the company, and how customers and employees are going to be engaged.

While being highly tech-savvy, leaders need to also understand and care about people and their wants and needs—customers, ecosystem partners, or employees within their own four walls. Market research isn't enough to let companies understand what customers want; leaders need to adopt a deeply human approach to gain privileged insights into customers. Leaders also need to engage employees with empathy and authenticity and to connect the company's purpose to what matters to them. All this requires leaders to see the human being behind the consumer or the workforce and show a real interest in what they want and aspire to.

Consider Saleh Mosaibah, the founding CEO of STC Pay. Mosaibah has been very deliberate about managing the tension between technology and humanism: "Having technology in the back of your mind is important because you need to know what's possible. But you must not be overwhelmed with technology's possibilities, whether it's mobile, smartphone, blockchain, AI, big data. While these have to be in the back of your mind, customers need to be front of your mind. Having this empathy with customers is critical."

During his tenure as CEO, Mosaibah was known for challenging everything traditional banks do and everything STC Pay does. He left no stone unturned. "You need to constantly challenge your thinking to fully realize what's possible in the digital era," he insists. When STC Pay was set up, it hired compliance people who were experts in anti–money laundering, combating terrorism financing, transaction monitoring, and much more. But, having traditional banking backgrounds, they had not been exposed to the possibilities of software and technology. They had used technology in very traditional ways. "When we showed them what's possible, their dreams became different. They started asking for more and more and more," Mosaibah remembers. A big part of STC Pay's compliance is now automated in a way that has never been done in any financial institution. "We achieved this by hiring industry experts and showing them what's possible in the digital era."

While being very tech-savvy, Mosaibah made sure that the company adopted a deeply human approach when developing their offerings. "We have created ten personas," he says. "Each one has a name, and we know what their day looks like from the minute they wake up, all the way to the minute they go to bed, how their week goes on, what they do on the weekend, when they get their salary, what they do when they get their salary." The company holds brainstorming sessions to determine how they can take care of Mohammed, the merchant, for example. "His pain point is that his employer always asks for invoices when he pays something; there are some trust issues between him and his employer."

All of STC Pay's designs start from personas. "We have to impersonate our users and live their life," Mosaibah insists. "Then we ask what we—STC Pay—can do for them. And once we've launched an initial solution, customers will then start using it and telling us exactly what they want. That's where the iterations start, where we continue adding services and features, all to meet the continuous updates of demands that we get from our users."

High-Integrity Politician

In today's ecosystem world, where companies and individuals with loosely aligned goals collaborate, being able to accrue support, negotiate, form coalitions, and overcome resistance is an essential leadership capability. Leaders need to make compromises, be flexible in tweaking their approach, go one step back to be able to move two steps forward. This is becoming increasingly important because ecosystem partners are beyond the reach of your command and control, and internal stakeholders of all ranks increasingly look to connect the work they do to their personal values. Leaders also need to convince large groups of stakeholders to go on the journey that their new place in the world requires, which will probably include redefining the portfolio, changing the underlying business model, redefining the organizational model, and changing shareholder expectations. Given the magnitude of the change ahead, leaders will need to be highly skilled at creating a wave of support and helping critical parties see their own pathway to change.

This is politics at its best—without the bad reputation it so often gets. Politics is the art of finding an agreed-upon path forward for groups of people with diverse, and sometimes divergent, interests. This kind of politics can succeed only if leaders maintain integrity and build trust in all their interactions. When people know that what they do contributes to a larger goal they care about and that leaders are going to remain true to that goal—even if it means making a compromise or taking a detour—people are going to join in on the journey and bet their careers or business on an idea they consider worth fighting for.

Given the importance of ecosystems for Microsoft's value creation, leaders at the company (whose transformation story we told in chapter 5) had to pay particular attention to the high-integrity politician leadership paradox. Microsoft's history is paved with legal disputes with many of its partners. When Satya Nadella became CEO, he knew he had to "hit refresh" on partnership practices:

> Microsoft already has the largest ecosystem of partners in the world. . . . My ultimate goal is to be the biggest platform provider underneath all of this entrepreneurial energy, with an unrelenting focus on creating economics opportunity for others. But if we want to convince millions of new companies around the world to bet on our platform, we need to start by earning their trust. . . . Trust is built by being consistent over time. It's built by being clear that there are places where we are going to compete to be best in class, and there are places where we can work together to add value for each other's customers. Trust has many other components as well—respect, listening, transparency, staying focused, and being willing to hit reset when necessary. We have to be principled about it.[3]

This shift in thinking at the top led Microsoft to start engaging its partners as allies in the commercial transformation program. It opened up to partners the same kind of training and development and capabilities that it offered to its internal employees. "We now offer full certifications in all of the solutions that we take to market for us, for partners and for customers themselves," says Nicola Hodson, vice president of Field Transformation in Global Sales, Marketing and Operations.

Reflecting on her learnings from Microsoft's commercial transformation, "Go slow to go fast" is the first one that came to Hodson's mind: "I work for an American software company—we like to move fast. But sometimes we need to move a little bit slower in order to get the outcome we want and not just bulldoze through it. Sometimes you can't go as fast as you want to because you have to bring everyone along. It sounds a little trite, but if you don't have a good coalition of support, it's probably not the right time to proceed. I've learned that." She continues, "I knew coming into this job that a lot of the role would be stakeholder management. But it was at least ten times more stakeholder management than I had anticipated. Building coalitions of support across organizational boundaries and slowing down in order to speed up—for me, was a big deal."

Humble Hero

These times call for leaders who are willing to make big decisions despite uncertainty and exude confidence with gravitas. The seven leadership imperatives require making bold decisions and committing to a path. It will not be enough to merely study and evaluate these imperatives. Transforming the company requires courage, decisiveness, and the stamina to stay true to the chosen direction even if things at first don't work out as planned.

Bold? Yes. Ego-driven? No. The world beyond digital rewards humility as much as it does heroics—indeed, the two traits need to go hand in hand. Leaders need humility to know what they don't know and to seek out people who can help. This applies to your cooperation with ecosystem partners, who may be better positioned to win in a certain area than your company. It also applies when you redesign your leadership team and add individuals who think and behave in ways that are very different from yours. And it applies when engaging people across the organization: given the speed of change and the complexity of the task ahead, no single leader and no single top team can aspire to have all the answers. Leaders need to be clear about the direction in which the company is headed, then make room for people who are closer to customers or more tech-savvy to bring that goal to life.

Frans van Houten exemplifies this humble hero leadership paradox. As told in chapter 2, van Houten took Philips through a series of transformations. He recalls, "The first four years were terrible. This was a very courageous transformation, where we as a leadership team could see the North Star, but not everybody else could. Shareholders didn't have a lot of confidence—after all, there was this historical perception of a thirty-year period in which Philips had been floundering. There was a lot of skepticism around us with people asking, 'What are you doing?'"

But van Houten and his top team stayed the course. Selling the lighting business was a pivotal moment in the company's transformation journey, as it started revealing the shape of the new Philips. "You could argue that exiting consumer electronics and TV and audio-video were necessities because they were loss-making businesses. But saying goodbye to lighting, which is our birthright, really changed the nature of who we were." These difficult decisions were key for refocusing Philips around health technology and putting the company on a trajectory of accelerated success: revenue grew, profitability increased, they pushed the limits of what was possible together with customers, and they were able to attract better talent. Van Houten's heroic leadership is clearly recognized by the organization. "I wouldn't have done it if it weren't for Frans. I think he clearly has the vision, and I really share that vision. I would never be here if there was a CEO that was not fully committed to where we're going," said Jeroen Tas, Philips's former chief innovation and strategy officer.

Yet van Houten has remained deeply humble. He's very open about the leadership journey he had to undertake to be up for the job and continues to prioritize his self-development. He is deeply committed to feedback and encourages his team to give him open feedback about what works well and what he could do better. He strives toward engaging people across the organization because it's clear to him that the world is way too complicated for him and his top team to have all the answers. His humility also shows in how he thinks about ecosystems: Philips is not looking to be in the lead all the time—it's OK to be a mere participant in an ecosystem if another player is better positioned to lead. Van Houten also insists on having representatives of select ecosystem partners join his top team meetings so they can continue to learn from those invaluable relationships.

Traditioned Innovator

Leaders in the digital age need to balance where the organization comes from and where it must go. In chapter 2, we discussed finding the hidden strengths of your organization and using those as one way to inform what your future place could be. Looking into the past can be powerful, and you may uncover aspects of your past that are no longer being used but that could be part of your future success.

But leaders can't just look to the past. Tradition would hold them back. They need to drive innovation and try out new things, more so now than at any time before. They need to have the courage to fail and need to allow others to fail as well. But they can't fall prey to the forces that pull companies into incoherence—forces that have grown given the increasing rate of change, the blurring of organizational boundaries, and the engagement of many more people across the organization in the shaping of the transformation journey. Experimentation and innovation, therefore, must not be unbounded—they must happen within the guardrails set by the company's place in the world. Otherwise, companies spread their resources thin, waste efforts on undertakings that don't allow them to wow the customers they care about, won't succeed at scaling up the required capabilities, and will not move the company forward in a concerted, coherent effort.

Eli Lilly's transformation through the years YZ, which we reviewed in chapter 6, and the leadership that the two CEOs—John Lechleiter and Dave Ricks—exhibited illustrate this paradox. When pressure from expiring patents mounted and the magnitude of the revenue at risk became clear, John Lechleiter, then CEO, decided to weather the crisis by staying true to the company's identity around innovative biopharmaceuticals, despite the advice from investors who wanted him to make a major acquisition, cut costs, and sell the animal health business. Lechleiter instead bet the company on its tradition of growth through innovation.

The years YZ were difficult times for employees, with many setbacks and challenges. The CEO led the organization through that period through purpose. Michael Overdorf, the former chief strategy officer, recalls. "John [Lechleiter]'s message has always been: 'Don't focus on us. We'll be fine. This is not the worst challenge this company has faced. We should be worried about the patients who aren't going to be helped, about the people who aren't going to have their lives transformed and their memories saved because we can't give them the drug they need.' This was an unbelievable message to send. It got people to say: 'All right, this is just another challenge. Let's rise to the occasion and save people's lives.'"

Staying committed to its tradition as an innovator didn't mean that the company was going to stand still. To the contrary. Indeed, Lilly had to greatly speed up its drug development, which back then required around thirteen years, one of the worst performances in the industry. The goal was to be industry-leading and get drugs to market in five years. To do so, as we described, John Lechleiter radically changed his top team, blew up the company's organization, and shook up R&D—and Lilly now has the fastest development times in many therapeutic areas. "This is not just incremental. It's a night-and-day difference," comments Overdorf.

Globally Minded Localist

It's much easier now than it used to be to reach customers on the other side of the globe, and people from far apart can work together more seamlessly. And even if your company is operating in one single country or region, the customers you are serving, your supply chain, and the people who work with you most probably have much more unique backgrounds and are influenced by a much more diverse set of factors than any time before. Successful leaders need to be students of the world with a deep understanding of broad societal trends, able to uncover common needs and wants of their customers, employees, and ecosystem partners and to scale relevant solutions and initiatives across their businesses.

But more than ever before, leaders also need to be deeply aware of and responsive to the situation and preferences of individual customers, cultural differences in their workforce, and the issues and nuances in the local communities and ecosystems in which they operate. Leaders in this complex environment must determine what they need to drive consistently across their company and where they can be flexible and allow for local tailoring. In fact, a company's ability to build privileged insights is greatly accelerated by leaders who personally reinforce the need to build strong relationships with individual customers all while innovating solutions that bring the best of what that organization sees in all of its markets.

Leaders at Inditex, for example, show how to negotiate this globally minded localist paradox. The company's success is based on deeply listening to consumers and understanding what they like, using these insights to uncover fashion trends that they are going to offer to the market, and offering them to the market more accurately and flexibly than any other company could. Sonia Fontán, director of the New York flagship Zara store, says, "I talk to our designers in Spain on a daily basis. The discussion may be 'This item was great, we sold all of it on the first day. We need more, please, we need more.' But it could also be 'We did not sell many of those neon bombers that we received yesterday.' But yesterday's information isn't indicative. It was raining, the store was empty. It's not that the customers did not like the things, it's just because of the weather."

Fontán has been running the store for ten years. She knows her customers: "You have different kinds of visitors during the year. In summer, for example, we have a lot of Brazilians, Argentinians visiting the stores. There are different customers in the middle of the week compared to on the weekends. The holidays are very special: Easter, Rosh Hashanah. When you've been in the store for a long time, you already know. And based on this expertise, you are going to change the layout in the store, the way you are going to show the collection."

Based on all those discussions with local experts together with the worldwide sales data they have about every item, designers in Spain are going to make sense of the world and create collections based on what they see customers liking or disliking. This results in sixty-five thousand different creations every year, which allows the company to send new collections to its stores twice a week.

Leaders at Inditex hold two fundamental beliefs about the fashion world that illustrate their global-local thinking. The first one is "Our customers' word is the correct one." While designers are really proud of their capabilities and achievements, they need to be humble and accept that the word of the customer—the individual local customer, wherever they are based—is the truth. The second belief is "Something that is beautiful in Tokyo is going to be beautiful everywhere— in New York or in Paris or in London." It allows you to find scale in the local tastes of millions of customers.

It may seem daunting to reconcile all of these leadership paradoxes. While you will probably feel confident and comfortable with some, others may feel like a challenge. (See "The Importance of the Six Paradoxes of Leadership—and Leaders' Biggest Gaps.") The good news is that not any one person needs to perfectly reconcile all of them. When you look at yourself and your team through the lens of these leadership paradoxes, you will most probably identify areas in which you are uniquely strong and others in which your limitations may be balanced by some of your team members who have complimentary skills. But you will unavoidably also uncover areas in which you need to step up to be an effective leader and transformer of your organization.

Reinventing Yourself and the Next Generation of Leaders

If you're already a leader, you know that time is one of your scarcest resources. You have to fight fires every day but still must find time to position the company for success in the longer term, while orchestrating the required transformation and staying on top of its execution. Too few executives find the time and peace of mind to step back and ponder their own leadership style and the development agenda they need to undertake. The successful leaders we studied, however, were all fully aware they had to work on their own development.

How can you start on your journey and develop the leadership characteristics your company needs you to have? While you're at it, how can you rethink leadership development at your company more broadly? After all, leadership capabilities aren't just important for you, they're also key for your current team and the next generation of leaders in your company—who will continue your transformation long after you've moved on.

Your first step will be to determine the leadership characteristics that are most important for your company. The six paradoxes that we have described above are all important—but depending on your company's strategy and its specific starting position, some traits will be more urgent than others.

The Importance of the Six Paradoxes of Leadership—and Leaders' Biggest Gaps

Strategy& conducted a survey in spring 2021 with over 500 participants from across regions and industries to gain insights into which leadership characteristics people consider most important to their company's future success, and how good their organizations' top leaders are at these characteristics. The results confirm what we learned in the research for this book, and what we have been observing in our client work with leaders for many years.

Indeed, each one of these six leadership paradoxes—and the twelve individual characteristics—is considered important or even critical to success by the vast majority of respondents. "Strategic executor" is the paradox that respondents rated the most important (with 96% of respondents considering both strategic and executor to be important or critical to the company's future success). Close behind were the "tech-savvy humanist" paradox (90%), "high-integrity politician" (84%), and "humble hero" (83%). The importance of the "globally minded localist" paradox was rated higher by companies with operations across more than one region (82% of respondents from companies with major operations in more than one region rated both being globally minded and localist as important or critical to success, compared with 67% of respondents from companies that operate in one region only). The "traditioned innovator" is an interesting paradox— with respondents generally considering being innovative more

We'd like to offer a few principles we're often using in our work with leaders and that can help you shape your development journey:

- **Be critically self-aware.** You need to have an honest conversation with yourself about what your strengths are, but also

Importance of and proficiency at the six paradoxes of leadership

■ Relevance: % of respondents indicating that both characteristics of the paradox are important or critical to the company's future success

■ Proficiency: % of respondents indicating that top leaders in their organization are good or best-in-class at both characteristics of the paradox

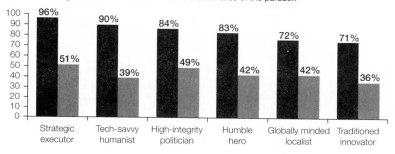

Source: Analysis from Strategy& survey of 515 participants, 2021.

important than being traditioned (but still 71% of respondents considering both to be important or critical to the company's success).

When it comes to leaders' proficiency at these characteristics, the survey revealed some significant gaps. For each of the six paradoxes, half or more than half of survey respondents consider top leaders at their organization to be not good at one or both of the two characteristics that make up that paradox. The gap is biggest for "traditioned innovator" (only 36% rate leaders to be good or best-in-class at both) and tech-savvy humanist" (39%), but still very significant for "globally minded localist" (42%), "humble hero" (42%), "high-integrity politician (49%), and "strategic executor" (51%).

where you have weaknesses. You may have a good sense of where you stand, but make sure you complement that with feedback from others, for example, your coach, your boss, your peers, your team members, your friends and family. (You can take our easy-to-use online diagnostic tool that helps you compare what you believe is most important against where you believe your largest gaps are. This assessment can be the beginning of a dialogue you have with your peers and mentors to develop your own plan. See strategyand.pwc.com/beyonddigital.)

- **Use your strengths to overcome your weaknesses.** If you're very disciplined but not particularly creative, use your discipline to create some down time where you can immerse yourself in some creative session. If you're organized but struggle with relationship building, develop a relationship map and relationship management plan and follow through using your proven systematic approach.

- **Study those who aren't you.** While many people feel most comfortable interacting with others who are like them, there's much more to learn from those who aren't. Look out for people who are great in areas you're not, observe what they're doing, and develop your own approach to learning, emulating and adapting changes that are right for you.

- **Seek the right experiences.** None of these characteristics can be built without experience. Throw yourself into situations that allow you to test and learn new behaviors. Many of those will take you out of your comfort zone, but there's no better way of learning than by doing.

Table 8-1 highlights some measures that leaders can take to build the knowledge and mindsets that are required to navigate each of the six paradoxes of leadership. This is not meant to be an exhaustive list; rather, it's a collection of ideas that will hopefully spark more ideas as you work through your development plan.

Your development plan will most certainly look different—but we hope that these examples will provide food for thought for when you

TABLE 8-1

Exemplary development measures along the six paradoxes

Leadership paradoxes	Exemplary measures to build knowledge and experiences	Exemplary measures to evolve mindsets and belief systems
Strategic executor	• Turn around a business • Work in a strategy role (e.g., chief strategy officer) • Manage a local operation or market • Work at a startup	• Get a coach to work with you and support your self-development • Throw yourself into experiences that challenge your comfort zone (e.g., public speaking opportunities, sports, adventure programs)
Tech-savvy humanist	• Do a tour of duty at a tech company (e.g., with an ecosystem partner) or technical department • Work for a nonprofit organization • Take online courses to build your knowledge in new areas	• Seek roles where you aren't in a leadership role, such as by volunteering and doing community service • Develop a reverse-mentoring relationship with someone who can teach you about areas you don't know
High-integrity politician	• Participate in an M&A deal • Support a post-merger integration • Engage in customer negotiations • Work with an ecosystem partner	• Make self-care a priority • Ask for and be open to feedback on specific behaviors (from colleagues, spouse, friends, etc.) • Seek to broaden your understanding of the issues impacting the world by learning about environmental and social issues
Humble hero	• Lead a business you don't know • Lead a cost improvement program, and resolve the difficult trade-offs • Take on a turnaround role	• Talk to friends and colleagues from different backgrounds to learn about their societal experiences and their views of the world
Traditioned innovator	• Do a tour of duty at a startup • Identify the true differentiators of your current organization	• Learn a new language • Learn about new cultures through their cuisines
Globally minded localist	• Gain international work experience (*live* in different countries, not just lead people there) • Get out of expat communities and into local associations • Lead a global capability team	

225

FIGURE 8-1

Worksheet to determine your own personal development plan

In order to position your company for success in the digital age, you will need to....

- Reimagine your company's place in the world
- Embrace and create value via ecosystems
- Build a system of privileged insights with your customers
- Make your organization outcome-oriented
- Invert the focus of your leadership team
- Reinvent the social contract with your people
- Disrupt your own leadership approach

This requires a new type of leader that embodies six seemingly paradoxical traits:	Importance of paradox to your success (H, M, L)	Your proficiency at this paradox (H, M, L)	Measures to build knowledge and experiences	Measures to evolve mindsets and belief systems
Strategic executor			. . . .	. . . .
Tech-savvy humanist				
High-integrity politician				
Humble hero				
Traditioned innovator				
Globally minded localist				

H=High, M=Medium, L=Low

Source: Strategy&.

fill in your own plan. You may want to use figure 8-1 as a worksheet to guide you.

Independent of how urgent your other priorities are, you will need to pay a lot of attention to and make time for your own development. Leadership development has always been important. After all, leaders are not superhumans—strengths and weaknesses are an inherent part of all of us. But given the size and nature of the transformation you will need to take your company through, some of your weak spots could significantly hinder your company's transformation.

Your own development is key to success. You need to make it a priority. You owe it to yourself, and you owe it to the companies and people you lead.

9

Accelerating Your Path to Success

The best time to plant a tree was twenty years ago.
The second best time is now.

—Chinese proverb

At this point, we hope you're both inspired by the opportunity ahead and cognizant of the meaningful gaps that may exist on your path toward a different level of value creation. The seven leadership imperatives we've outlined and the stories of the twelve exemplars provide a road map and should give you confidence that you, too, can secure your company's place in the world beyond digital. At the same time, we recognize that the seven imperatives may seem overwhelming. While each on its own could potentially be managed in the course of normal business, executing all of them together—or even a number of them—will require significant, sustained effort. There is no equivocating about this: the transformation of how you create value will not happen overnight—it is a multiyear journey.

All the statistics show that large-scale transformation programs often fall short of delivering on their promise. Big decisions that were meant to change the direction of the company get weakened because the future is felt to be too uncertain; options need to be hedged. Short-term performance pressures frequently divert attention and funding from the longer term. Executives, considering their remaining tenure, sometimes delay action. Legacy businesses keep getting the lion's share of the company's energy and resources. And organizations struggle under the weight of all the initiatives that were undertaken in the past and that disappointed.

So how do you succeed where others have failed?

You need to answer a series of questions: Do you believe in the future you've articulated? Are you going to hold your team and your organization accountable to deliver this future? Are you going to break through the challenges you will face—or let them encumber you? Are you going to accelerate and transform—or retreat to incremental steps?

Your most important task will be to provide the decisiveness and honesty required for each of the seven leadership imperatives. If you compromise now, as you start the process, you'll send a signal that will undercut the power of everything you attempt from here on.

So, here are some mechanisms that can help you stay on the road that will get you from where you are today to where you want to be.

Mechanisms to Secure Your Path

Our experience is that organizations can easily focus on perceived areas of great urgency when embarking on a transformation—for example, racing to catch up with new products or services that competitors have launched. But urgency won't sustain you, and a series of separate initiatives won't get you where you want to go.

You need to begin by stepping back and working your way through the seven imperatives: reimagining your place in the world, your ecosystem(s), your privileged insights, your organization, your leadership team, your social contract with employees, and your own leadership style. While you may execute the seven imperatives in stages, it is important to be clear that they come as a package. Do just one or two, and you are likely to fall short or suffer through more pain than needed.

The seven imperatives have to be executed as a coherent effort. You cannot expect the company to work in new ways if you don't engage people and change how you organize them to work. You cannot expect leaders to simply do more or change overnight; you must first reposition the leadership team. And you clearly cannot get anywhere if you don't redefine your place in the world, including how it fits with others in your ecosystem (who will not be sitting still while you decide what to do).

The clearer you are about the seven imperatives as a package at the start, the more you will understand what it really takes to succeed and the more energy you will generate to power the effort. But you and your team must be brutally honest about the gaps that exist in any of the seven imperatives—not doing so is one of the biggest reasons for failure that we see in our research and our work with clients.

We borrow an expression from a colleague of ours, Gary Neilson, coauthor of the book *Results*. He says that, in transformations, it is critical to have "amnesty for the past."[1] We must allow all of our executives to focus on being clear about what is needed to succeed, rather than why they may not have addressed a gap before. If the list of gaps is long, so be it. You will have time to sequence, prioritize, and adjudicate tradeoffs to fill those gaps. But you cannot start out with a myopic view. You can't convince yourself, or let others convince you, that a real gap somehow doesn't exist or can be easily covered.

Even with great intentions, honesty and passion, you will, of course, make mistakes along the way, so we asked the leadership teams we studied to share the most important lessons they learned from the injuries and scars they sustained, as well as all the things they did right. While each of their stories had personal nuances, the commonalities were stunningly simple, yet enlightening. Here are the key lessons to consider as you take the next steps.

Partner with the board of directors on the imperatives. Undertaking a transformation carries significant risk for leaders. What if some of the assumptions about the market are incorrect? What if short-term performance takes too much of a hit? And what if the organization just doesn't have the capacity to get to the destination?

A number of the CEOs we interviewed said it was key to their success that they engaged the board of directors up front around the way value would be created, the destination they were seeking, and the connected imperatives that would get them there. Boards often have a longer view of the organization and are likely to be considering these very questions. They may also be getting pressure themselves from outsiders, or applying pressure to management for some form of transformation. When you have conversations with the board, you will want to focus on the vision you have, the challenges of the current model and possible alternatives, the capabilities of the organization, and what could be achieved by going through the transformation.

Almost all the leaders we spoke to focused on the importance of being consistent about the goals as they went through the journey—especially when times were challenging. In some instances, the composition of the board itself was revised to bring new insights and energy. In others, each board meeting began with a recap of the progress against the total journey, helping to create ownership and support by the board. Regardless of the mechanism, creating clarity with the board about *both* the destination *and* the path to get there is key to powering and sustaining the needed change.

Engage key shareholders. Engaging key shareholders helps create the room for transformation, particularly if there will be economic tradeoffs such as short-term pain for longer-term success. Helping these shareholders understand the big problem you're going to solve, why you are uniquely positioned to solve this problem, how you are going to get there, what the risks are in transforming (and in not transforming), and the expected impact on your company's performance is powerful. In several instances, CEOs and CFOs told us they created an additional, unexpected drive for change when they shared the story of their planned transformation, including the time it would take, the uncertainties involved, and the multitude of efforts needed. While the executives thought they might be criticized for losing focus on quarterly earnings, they discovered that key shareholders are equally motivated by bold change, even when that comes with higher risk, and similarly do not want companies to mortgage the future for today's benefit. Transformation is material for shareholders, and they expect companies to act *now* to secure the future.

Prioritize around customers. Your place in the world, the privileged insights you build into your customers and end users, the role you play in your ecosystems are all about creating value for your customers. Solving real customer problems and addressing real customer needs are the raison d'être for any transformation. Therefore, anchoring your change efforts in customers is the best way to create momentum. That is what gets everyone excited: employees, leaders, shareholders, ecosystem partners, and, of course, customers themselves. Before you begin mapping out how you can improve efficiency in the back office and cut costs by implementing new technology, focus your energy on how to turbocharge the differentiating capabilities that are at the heart of how you create value for customers. Build your digitization efforts around solutions that touch customers and around the front line of the organization that serves them. These frontline efforts often serve as the earliest tangible proof of the new value you can create. In many cases, they provide the stories around which you can catalyze action. Seeing how to win by making a difference for customers energizes people to change far more than initiatives you may undertake internally or corporate goals to "grow revenue" or "gain market share." Even the leadership teams we spoke to who started their transformation efforts by focusing on solving an internal challenge emphasized the importance of anchoring the work in how it made a tangible difference to winning in the market.

Focus on capabilities and outcomes, not digital initiatives. Most of the differentiating capabilities you will need to build will inevitably require some technology. Start with blueprinting the amazing outcomes of each capability—and detail every element that must change, including data, systems, people, and process. When you do digitize, don't claim victory once a new system or tool is in production—there is a lot more that needs to be done in terms of changing processes and upskilling people. Setting your targets around the end outcomes you are seeking to achieve (e.g., improved customer service, better forecast accuracy, improved business predictability) helps focus the whole team on delivering those outcomes instead of declaring victory for simply putting a piece of technology in place. An outcome focus also helps ensure that your investments are appropriately channeled and that your cross-functional teams feel a sense of mutual accountability to ensure the success of your investments.

Invest in your people from the start. The seven leadership imperatives put a lot of emphasis on engaging your people—the leaders around you and the people within your organization. The leadership teams we interviewed almost universally agreed about the importance of investing early on to engage people and power the change. However, the topic of engagement can often be picked up late or buried under a "change management" effort that is delegated. While the initial temptation can be to focus more on developing new digital solutions and creating new lines of business, these often cannot scale up fast enough to deliver competitive advantage. Meanwhile, employees seek to make a difference, and efforts to motivate them toward your new place can pay large dividends and counter what often becomes a fear that the change will leave them behind.

Helping your people transform as you develop the future of the company creates momentum that can make the change self-driving. Indeed, the most successful executives we interviewed stressed the importance of making sure people know that they are valued and said that helping them build their digital acumen, their skills, and their adaptability was more valuable than investing millions in developing new solutions. The new solutions, the new ways of working with customers, and the new ways of creating significant incremental value could only scale up meaningfully once the organization was ready to drive forward. In fact, some leaders commented on how empowering people to develop new skills led to new solutions and ways of working that would have otherwise taken significantly longer and cost significantly more. Investing in your people's and your ecosystem's ability to power the change early on is a catalyst for creating the competitive advantage you want.

Your people include your leaders, and we cannot emphasize enough how important it is to have the right leaders and the right leadership team in place to manage the transformation ahead. You must have the right leaders, with the right mindset around collective effort (no transformation we've seen comes as a result of individualist behavior alone). You also must have the right mechanisms in place to give the leadership team the space to drive all of the changes. Otherwise, it's hard to imagine how you will be successful.

Separate the old from the new. Fixing the legacy business while at the same time standing up the new one may be more than one team can do. So, several companies adopt an operating model that separates the old from the new.

This can take many forms. Some put in place two separate teams: one figures out how to make the most of the legacy business, how to sustain significant cash generation, and potentially how to sell it off; the other focuses on how to develop the new business, how to build the required capabilities, how to create value with the new ecosystems. Other companies spin off or sell off the businesses that aren't core. While the approaches may differ, the goal is the same: allowing the new business to develop without being held back by too much legacy.

The companies and leadership teams we studied emphasized enabling the new model to thrive and develop with its own rules. Constraining new business models and solutions with the structures, performance metrics, and systems of the old was universally seen as a sure path to failure. While it was of course helpful to be fed capabilities from the legacy business, the new ways of thinking and operating required for success could not be captured under the legacy models. New operating models were necessary—even if the changes were staged over time to allow for a stable transition from the legacy model to the future. Citigroup would not have been able to stand up the new bank without separating off legacy businesses into Citi Holdings. And STC Pay would not have been able to act like a speedboat had it stayed too close to the mother ship.

Some other companies went even further in clearly delineating the new from the old. They used trigger events and inorganic mechanisms to clearly signal a break from the past and a focus on the future. These changes helped challenge both internal and external stakeholders to question long-held beliefs about how to create value. Philips's divestment of its foundational lighting business to focus on transforming health care was perhaps one of the starkest examples of declaring a break from the past. This very visible symbol of change generated new conversations and energy within the company hallways, and with investors, about what it would take to succeed. The break changed how people thought about the company and produced fresh focus on the future.

Regardless of the mechanism chosen, the resounding lesson learned was to move fast and early to separate the old from the new. No one we spoke to wished they had taken more time to stake out and scale up the new direction. Making a clear, quick break generated momentum. This does not mean that you do not honor, appreciate, or most importantly leverage the past. The legacy has a valued place, but the new simply cannot thrive in its shadow.

. . .

Aspiring to shape the future is part of our character as business leaders. Avoiding incrementalism is where real leadership is required. You already know you have a tremendous responsibility in your role. This is your opportunity to solve what most have not—delivering a meaningful future, addressing a fundamental customer or societal challenge, and actually seeing it through.

In the many moments where your own voice, and certainly that of others, will say, "We cannot get there," "This is not for us," "We're already successful," "We have a plan already," and the myriad other comments that incite incrementalism, we know you will be reminded of the great stories of transformation and of the great need for you, at that moment, to help your people see the potential in a world beyond digital.

The legacy you leave for yourself, your organization, and the rest of us depends on it.

Appendix

Puretone Ways to Play

To help challenge your thinking about potential ways in which you could add value to your customers and customers' customers, we've outlined below a set of common strategic archetypes for creating value—we call these *puretones*. These usually wind up being critical elements in companies' ultimate value proposition and can help you understand if such a value proposition may be relevant for your business.

Some of these puretone ways to play have become more prevalent in the recent past (for example, platform providers and experience providers). Others have lost in importance (for example, category leaders or consolidators). Table A-1 shows the puretone ways to play we have uncovered in our research, lists a few examples of companies that exhibit those ways to play, and discusses how the new competitive dynamic of the digital age has impacted each of these plays. You can use this list as a starting point when setting out to identify places in the world that could be relevant for your company.

Companies generally don't create value according to just one puretone way to play—they typically mix elements of several puretones

TABLE A-1

List of puretones

Puretone	Definition	Examples	Evolution in the beyond digital age
Aggregator	Provides the convenience and simplicity of one-stop shopping	• Amazon • eBay • Airbnb • Travel agencies • W. W. Grainger	*Changing:* The digital age has made aggregating easier and highly valuable, but aggregators often need to also provide other benefits, particularly around curation of content and offerings to help customers make sense of all the offerings that are available.
Category leader	Maintains top market share in a category and uses that position to shape and influence downstream channels and upstream supply markets, gaining leverage and customer loyalty	• Coca-Cola • Frito-Lay • Intel • L'Oréal • Starbucks • Walmart	*Losing in importance:* Competing on size alone is no longer an option in the beyond digital age. Companies generally need to differentiate more than the influence they have over a sector, unless barriers to entry like governmental influence are very high.
Consolidator	Dominates an industry through acquisitions ("rolling up an industry") to provide either a value benefit to consumers or access to a platform with products and services that otherwise would not be possible	• Danaher • GE	*Losing in importance:* This way to play does not—on its own—provide immediate value to customers. With lower hurdles to partnering in the increasingly frictionless environment, companies do not necessarily have to acquire to amass scale. Similarly, just creating economic benefit through scale does not create a strong value proposition, but this strategy may be a component of a customer-focused play where scale is either required or synergies are invested in real differentiation.

Customizer	Leverages insight and market intelligence to offer tailored products or services	• Burger King (with its "Have it your way" campaign) • Companies that build electronics and computer systems to order • Inditex	*Gaining in importance:* Customers expect their needs and wants to be met at a much more granular level, and technology has enabled companies to produce profitably at much lower scale.
Disintermediator	Helps customers bypass unreachable or more expensive distribution channels and parts of the value chain, thereby providing access to otherwise inaccessible services and products	• Uber (disintermediates dispatchers and medallion holders) • Waze (disintermediates map-makers)	*Gaining in importance:* Technology enables the cooperation of players that previously required an intermediary.
Experience provider	Builds enjoyment, engagement, and emotional attachment through strong brands or experiences	• Apple • Hotel chains with a design-based or specialty value proposition • Sports car makers • Starbucks	*Gaining in importance:* Customer experience is so important now that it sometimes seems as though every company has to have some aspect of an experience provider. For those that choose to compete primarily in this way, expectations are high.
Fast follower	Leverages foundations laid by innovators to quickly introduce competing offerings, often at greater value or to a broader base of consumers	• Generic pharmaceutical manufacturers • Google (with Android) • Hyundai • Chinese *shanzhai* (innovative "knockoff" manufacturers)	*Losing in importance:* This may be a component of those that choose to compete as a low-cost provider, but merely copying products may not be enough to differentiate given the solutions that customers increasingly want.
Innovator	Introduces creative products or services to the market	• Apple • Inditex • Leading-edge biotech companies • Procter & Gamble	*Unchanged:* This way to play is still very relevant. In order to win, innovators need to excel at gaining privileged insights into customers to guide their innovation efforts.

(continued)

Puretone	Definition	Examples	Evolution in the beyond digital age
Integrator	Assembles or curates related products and services into a bundled offering	• General contractors bundling services from various suppliers to deliver a new or renovated house • Hospitals that integrate various doctors, medical services, and clinics into a care system to serve patients • Travel agents that bundle flights, ground transport, hospitals, tour guides, etc., into one offering	*Gaining in importance:* Many ecosystems are enabled by an integrator that provides a hassle-free experience to customers by bundling products and services from multiple providers into one offering. Integrators sometimes disintermediate, but go several steps further in curating, directing, and assembling a set of products and services and bundle them together for simplicity to the end customer.
Orchestrator	Enables multiple ecosystem participants to collaborate to deliver higher value to customers	• Komatsu • Network of doctors who refer patients to one another	*Gaining in importance:* Enables ecosystems to deliver more value to customers by better coordinating what individual contributors do without fully integrating services. Unlike integrators, orchestrators do not necessarily bundle products and services, but focus more on coordinating the entire ecosystem to deliver new solutions that had not previously existed.
Platform provider	Operates and oversees a shared resource or infrastructure	• Amazon • Facebook • Microsoft • New York Stock Exchange	*Gaining in importance:* Many ecosystems are enabled by a platform provider. Companies can use platform providers to access table stakes capabilities without actually owning them.
Premium player	Offers high-end products or services	• Herman Miller • Luxury automakers such as BMW • LVMH • Premium hotel chains such as Ritz-Carlton	*Losing in importance:* It's more difficult now to exist purely as a premium player without offering other value. Premium players increasingly need the associated experience or other benefits to continue to differentiate.

Player	Description	Examples	Future outlook
Regulation navigator	Offers access to otherwise unreachable products and services by managing within government rules and oversight and by influencing them	• Health insurance companies • Regulated utility companies • China National Offshore Oil Corporation (government-owned) • Industrial and Commercial Bank of China (government-owned) • Some trading companies (Mitsui)	*Unchanged:* These players still exist (and thrive) in markets that aren't open.
Reputation player	As a trustworthy provider, charges a premium or gains privileged access to customers	• Costco • Financial services companies with reputations for probity • Tata Group • Seventh Generation • Volvo (Geely Automotive)	*Unchanged:* Reputation and trust are important for customers to open up and for companies to gain privileged insights.
Risk absorber	Mitigates or pools market risk for its customers	• Commodity hedge funds • New hybrid health-care providers-payers, following the Kaiser Permanente model • Many insurance companies	*Unchanged:* Risk absorbers are still needed to help others extend entrepreneurially or help them navigate uncertainty.
Solutions provider	Provides bundled products and services that fully address customer needs	• Philips • Hitachi • Microsoft	*Gaining in importance:* Any B2B company and many B2C players likely have to consider being a solutions provider. Many will also be platform providers because they need to fit together disparate technologies and practices, including those from customers and potentially even competitors.
Value player	Offers lowest prices or tremendous value for comparable products and services	• IKEA • JetBlue • McDonald's • Ryanair • Southwest Airlines • Walmart	*Unchanged:* Successful value players use the full suite of digital tools and technologies to take out cost across the entire value chain.

to create a winning value proposition. Consider IKEA, the largest home furnishing company in the world. It is a value player, for sure, striving to offer affordable home furnishing. But it is an experience provider as well through the unique retail atmosphere it creates, including Swedish-style restaurants, playgrounds, and kids' bath-rooms. Don't be surprised if you see companies appear as examples of more than one puretone.

Notes

Chapter 1

1. Find out more about how companies build and leverage differentiating capabilities to create sustainable advantage in Paul Leinwand and Cesare Mainardi, with Art Kleiner, *Strategy That Works: How Winning Companies Close the Strategy-to-Execution Gap* (Boston: Harvard Business Review Press, 2016). For more on our research on how companies create sustained value, see www.strategyand.pwc.com/gx/en/unique-solutions /capabilities-driven-strategy/approach.html.

2. Shep Hyken, "Customer Loyalty and Retention Are in Decline," *Forbes*, October 13, 2019, www.forbes.com/sites/shephyken/2019/10/13 /customer-loyalty-and-retention-are-in-decline.

3. Business Roundtable, "Business Roundtable Redefines the Purpose of a Corporation to Promote 'An Economy That Serves All Americans,'" August 19, 2019, www.businessroundtable.org/business-roundtable -redefines-the-purpose-of-a-corporation-to-promote-an-economy-that -serves-all-americans.

4. Ernest Hemingway, *The Sun Also Rises* (New York: Scribner, 1926).

5. This and other quotations from executives in the companies we studied are from interviews conducted by the authors from 2018 through 2021. Titles are as of spring 2021.

6. "Inditex 1Q20 Sales Drop Limited to 44% Despite up to 88% of Stores Closed," Inditex.com, June 10, 2020, www.inditex.com/article ?articleId=648065.

7. For more on the research behind this approach, see www.strategyand .pwc.com/gx/en/unique-solutions/capabilities-driven-strategy/approach .html.

Chapter 2

1. www.philips.com/a-w/research/vision-and-mission.html.

2. "Hitachi's Challenges," interview with Hiroaki Nakanishi in Diamond *Harvard Business Review*, July 2016, https://www.dhbr.net/articles/-/4325.

3. Paul Leinwand and Cesare Mainardi, *The Essential Advantage: How to Win with a Capabilities-Driven Strategy* (Boston: Harvard Business Review Press, 2011).

4. The right to win is an important concept we described in Leinwand and Mainardi, *The Essential Advantage*. You can find an exercise that guides you through your right-to-win assessment at www.strategyand.pwc.com /gx/en/unique-solutions/capabilities-driven-strategy/right-to-win-exercise .html.

Chapter 3

1. "Komatsu Partners with Propeller," *Modern Contractor Solutions*, August 2018, mcsmag.com/komatsu-partners-with-propeller; "Japan's Komatsu Selects NVIDIA as Partner for Deploying AI to Create Safer, More Efficient Construction Sites," NVIDIA press release, December 12, 2017; nvidianews.nvidia.com/news/japans-komatsu-selects-nvidia-as-partner-for -deploying-ai-to-create-safer-more-efficient-construction-sites; "Komatsu Partners with Advantech for AIoT Heavy Duty Construction Equipment," Advantech website, April 1, 2020, www.advantech.com/resources/case -study/komatsu-partners-with-advantech-for-aiot-heavy-duty-construction -equipment; Patrick Cozzi, "Cesium and Komatsu Partner on Smart Construction Digital Twin," Cesium.com, March 10, 2020, www.cesium .com/blog/2020/03/10/smart-construction/.

2. "The History of Smart Construction," Komatsu website, October 16, 2019, www.komatsu.eu/en/news/the-history-of-smart-construction; "Everyday Drone Survey," Komatsu website, https://smartconstruction .komatsu/catalog_en/construction/everyday_drone.html.

3. "Realizing the Safe, Highly Productive and Clean Worksite of the Future: Launch of 'Smart Construction Digital Transformation,'" Komatsu website, March 10, 2020, home.komatsu/en/press/2020/management /1205354_1840.html.

4. "Patient First: How Karolinska University Hospital Is Transforming to Meet Future Demands of Healthcare," Philips website, www.philips.com /a-w/about/news/archive/case-studies/20190128-patient-first-how -karolinska-university-hospital-is-transforming-to-meet-future-demands-of -healthcare.html.

5. Satya Nadella, *Hit Refresh* (New York: Harper Collins, 2017), 124.

6. U. N. Sushma, "Titan Opens India's First Karigar Centre at Hosur to 'Transform the Lives of Goldsmiths,'" *Times of India*, February 22, 2014, timesofindia.indiatimes.com/articleshow/30810718.cms.

Chapter 4

1. Eric Cox, "How Adobe Drives Its Own Transformation," *Adobe Blog*, March 17, 2019, theblog.adobe.com/how-adobe-drives-its-own -transformation/.

2. "Digital Transformation Is in Our DNA," www.adobe.com/ch_de /customer-success-stories/adobe-experience-cloud-case-study.html.

3. Dan Murphy, "Saudi Arabia's STC Pay Eyes Rapid Gulf Expansion After Billion-Dollar Valuation," *CNBC*, November 23, 2020, www.cnbc.com /2020/11/23/saudi-arabias-stc-pay-eyes-rapid-gulf-expansion.html.

4. Paloma Díaz Soloaga and Mercedes Monjo, "Caso Zara: La empresa donde todo comunica," *Harvard Deusto Marketing y Ventas* 101 (November– December 2010): 60–68; and Zeynep Ton, Elena Corsi, and Vincent Dessain, "Zara: Managing Stores for Fast Fashion," case 9-610-042 (Boston: Harvard Business School, rev. January 19, 2010).

Chapter 5

1. Jon Katzenbach, Gretchen Anderson, and James Thomas, *The Critical Few: Working with Your Culture to Change It* (San Francisco: Berrett-Koehler, 2018).

2. The Katzenbach Center, www.strategyand.pwc.com/gx/en/insights /katzenbach-center.html.

3. Katzenbach, Anderson, and Thomas, *The Critical Few*.

Chapter 6

1. William R. Kerr and Alexis Brownell, "Transformation at Eli Lilly & Co. (A)," case 9-817-070 (Boston: Harvard Business School, November 7, 2016).

2. Kerr and Brownell, "Transformation at Eli Lilly & Co. (A)."

3. Doug J. Chung, "Commercial Sales Transformation at Microsoft," case 9-519-054 (Boston: Harvard Business School Publishing, January 28, 2019).

4. Greg Satell, "The Truth about Diverse Teams," *Inc.*, April 22, 2018, www.inc.com/greg-satell/science-says-diversity-can-make-your-team-more -productive-but-not-without-effort.html.

5. Lu Hong and Scott E. Page, "Groups of Diverse Problem Solvers Can Outperform Groups of High-Ability Problem Solvers," *PNAS* 101, no. 46 (2004): 16385–16389, sites.lsa.umich.edu/scottepage/wp-content/uploads /sites/344/2015/11/pnas.pdf.

6. Satya Nadella, *Hit Refresh* (New York: Harper Collins, 2017), 81.

Chapter 7

1. Tomislav Mihaljevic, "Tiered Teams Solve Problems in Real Time," Consult QD website, October 5, 2018, consultqd.clevelandclinic.org/tiered -teams-solve-problems-in-real-time/.

Notes

2. Satya Nadella, *Hit Refresh* (New York: Harper Collins, 2017), 104.

3. PwC 24th Annual Global CEO Survey 2021, www.pwc.com/gx/en/ceo-agenda/ceosurvey/2021.html.

4. William R. Kerr and Alexis Brownell, "Transformation at Eli Lilly & Co. (A)," case 9-817-070 (Boston: Harvard Business School, November 7, 2016).

Chapter 8

1. Paul Leinwand and Cesare Mainardi, with Art Kleiner, *Strategy That Works: How Winning Companies Close the Strategy-to-Execution Gap* (Boston: Harvard Business Review Press, 2016), chapter 7.

2. Blair H. Sheppard, *Ten Years to Midnight: Four Urgent Global Crises and Their Strategic Solutions* (San Francisco: Berrett-Koehler Publishers, 2020).

3. Satya Nadella, *Hit Refresh* (New York: Harper Collins, 2017), 134.

Chapter 9

1. Gary Neilson and Bruce Pasternack, *Results: Keep What's Good, Fix What's Wrong, and Unlock Great Performance* (New York: Crown Business, 2005).

Index

Note: Page numbers followed by *f* refer to figures; page numbers followed by *t* refer to tables.

Acknowledgments

People often ask us how we had time to write a book and conduct all of the research that supports our findings. The reality is that we are very fortunate to have brilliant and unbelievably supportive colleagues here at PwC and Strategy& who make this easier and who are integral to our ability to provide meaningful and pragmatic advice to leaders.

We are also incredibly fortunate to have worked with so many great clients over the years—companies and individuals who have inspired us through the brave decisions they have taken and the ambitious transformation journeys they have pursued, and who have always dared us to dig deeper to find better solutions to some of their most pressing opportunities and challenges.

This book wouldn't have been possible without the twelve companies that agreed to be part of the research effort. Thank you to the leadership teams (and the many helping hands in the background) at Adobe, Citigroup, Cleveland Clinic, Eli Lilly, Hitachi, Honeywell, Inditex, Komatsu, Microsoft, Philips, STC Pay, and Titan for allowing us to learn from what they have done—their successes and setbacks—so that we can share those lessons with others. One might wonder why they are willing to share their secrets to success. We believe that, among many reasons, they see the many challenges the world is facing and the problems waiting to be solved—and want to make a contribution this way. After all, success isn't a zero-sum game.

While these companies provided incredible learnings, one particular individual led all this research—maintaining a very high bar for the quality of our methodology—and ensured that this book and the related article series met that standard: our colleague and PwC

Acknowledgments

Director Nadia Kubis. Nadia is both brilliant and incredibly collaborative, and she is deeply committed to representing the research accurately and powerfully—a combination of skills not found in many. Her expertise in producing high-impact thought leadership is unmatched in our experience. We were extremely fortunate to have her drive the program, and it made a challenging experience highly rewarding and fun. Thank you, Nadia.

The book also benefited from many other great individuals along the way. Thanks to Rob Norton, who conducted the early research, identifying important learnings, and supported many of the first drafts of this book, and to Paul Carroll, who helped pull together the final manuscript with great stories and a wonderful ability to help sharpen the language, logic, and impact. Early in the process, we had fantastic guidance from our friend Art Kleiner, who shepherded many of the previous *Harvard Business Review* articles and books in this series, and we always received great advice and counsel from Tom Stewart, whose wonderful guest appearances made the content richer and our working sessions more fun.

One person is responsible for getting us started with this project: our colleague Mike Connolly. One year after the publication of our previous book, *Strategy That Works*, Mike said something like, "OK, that was awesome; what's next?" and pushed us to focus on providing much-needed advice for companies navigating the changes on the horizon. This launched what we called back then the "Leadership in a Digital Age" research project. Thank you, Mike, for not letting us rest.

We are grateful for support from Bob Pethick, who led the program that brought this thought leadership to life, and who together with Joachim Rotering, Allen Webb, and Martina Sangin helped shape this effort. They deserve credit for urging us to adopt a new thought leadership model, moving from "write a book, follow up with a series of articles" to "write a series of articles that lead to a book so that you get your findings to executives as soon as possible"—an approach that has worked really well with already highly read HBR articles including "Digitizing Isn't the Same as Digital Transformation" and "6 Leadership Paradoxes for the Post-Pandemic Era." They each pushed us in different ways to improve the quality and relevance of our ideas.

We are indebted to PwC leadership for supporting this project and seeing its potential. We particularly want to thank Kevin Burrowes, Mohamed Kande, Bob Moritz, Tim Ryan, Martin Scholich, and Blair Sheppard, who championed this effort to be true to our commitment to making a difference in society.

The PwC partnership is incredibly powerful, and that is seen in the tremendous engagement of partners who read the manuscript (some of them several times) and provided great perspective (and often tough feedback, which is exactly what we had hoped for and needed)—thank you, Nithin Bendore, Ian Kahn, Dan Priest, and Blair Sheppard. Thank you, Ann-Denise Grech, for your invaluable feedback about both big picture items and the smallest details. And thank you, Olaf Acker, Deniz Caglar, Vinay Couto, Carrie Duarte, Peter Gassmann, Paul Gaynor, Ann Johnston, Mohamed Kande, Colm Kelly, Colin Light, Scott Likens, Cornel Nolte, Bhushan Sethi, Matt Siegel, and Carol Stubbings, for the inspiring discussions and for letting us build on your expertise and wisdom around some of the important topics covered in this book.

We are highly appreciative to Gerald Adolph and DeAnne Aguirre—these two have a deep history in client work and are now retired from the firm, but they took the time not only to go through the manuscript in great detail but to provide highly impactful guidance that holistically made this a better book. It also helped that both have been our mentors for many years and knew just how to give us the right feedback. You hopefully know this already, but it has to be said again: you both are awesome.

Many of our colleagues played critical roles in helping us research and reflect on the companies we studied. Gary Ahlquist, Scott Brown,

Acknowledgments

Siddharth Doshi, Dan Elisha, Jad Hajj, Dave Hoffman, Taizo Iwashima, Yoshiyuki Kishimoto, Bob Long, Chuck Marx, Alison McNerney, Alison Millar, Patrick Pugh, Nissa Mohomed Shariff, Gurpreet Singh, Ayumi Suda, and Andrew Tipping: this body of research wouldn't exist without you.

We also had support from a great marketing team to ensure these ideas would reach the market. Thank you to the global marketing team and the many talented people in countries around the globe for all the helping hands. We would like to thank Geri Gibson in particular, who's been the spider in the web for everything related to marketing these ideas.

Our relationship with Harvard Business Review Press started more than 13 years ago, when they saw the potential of our ideas around capabilities. They have been a wonderful partner through all four books and the many articles and events we have worked on together. Melinda Merino has been there from the beginning, always asking the right questions to focus the work. Joining Melinda this time was editor Kevin Evers. Both were incredibly positive, thoughtful, constructive, and excellent collaborators. This book also benefited from the quality of attention of Sally Ashworth, Akila Balasubramaniyan, Julie Devoll, Lindsey Dietrich, Stephani Finks, Brian Galvin, Erika Heilman, Alexandra Kephart, Julia Magnuson, Ella Morrish, Allison Peter, Jon Shipley, and Felicia Sinusas. Thank you also to Amy Bernstein and Sarah Moughty for helping us get some of our ideas to the world ahead of the book.

It must not go without saying that this book builds on our previous three with HBR Press, all coauthored with Cesare Mainardi. His vision for the realm of strategic thinking—and indeed the practice of strategy consulting—helped build a solid foundation for *Beyond Digital*. Thank you for your great partnership over the years.

Nothing much would get done without the people who support us at the "office" and have helped in many ways: Cindy Funk, Yvonne Lauppe, and Marlo McMillan-Okuadido. Thank you for scheduling the meetings, and rescheduling them, and rescheduling them again. We would be lost without you.

The most thanks, however, go to our respective families, who were so incredibly patient with the late nights and weekend calls needed to complete this work. Their support wasn't just in helping find the space for us to do this but in doing gymnastics to make schedules work and most importantly for constantly encouraging and championing us on this journey. Thank you: Te, Cia, and G. G.; Meredith, Priyanka, Alik, and Amma.

—Paul Leinwand, Mahadeva Matt Mani

About the Authors

Paul Leinwand is Global Managing Director, Capabilities-Driven Strategy and Growth, with Strategy&, PwC's strategy consulting business. He is a principal with PwC US. Leinwand serves global clients through large-scale strategy and transformation efforts. He currently leads the US firm's business at the intersection of consumer and health, working with large consumer organizations and health-care systems.

Leinwand has coauthored a series of books published by Harvard Business Review Press, including *Strategy That Works* (2016), *The Essential Advantage* (2010), and *Cut Costs and Grow Stronger* (2009). He has also coauthored many articles on strategy and leadership with *Harvard Business Review*, *strategy+business*, and the *Wall Street Journal*, including "Why Are We Here?," "The Coherence Premium," "Digitizing Isn't the Same as Digital Transformation," "6 Leadership Paradoxes for the Post-Pandemic Era," "The Cure for the Not-For-Profit Crisis," and "Ask an Expert: How Do I Become a CEO?"

Leinwand is an adjunct professor of strategy at Northwestern's Kellogg School of Management and has served as an adviser to many nonprofit organizations. He holds a master's degree in management with distinction from Kellogg and a bachelor of arts in political science from Washington University in St. Louis.

Mahadeva Matt Mani leads the PwC/Strategy& transformation platform. He is a principal with PwC US. Mani is a senior adviser to companies and leaders across industries on business model transformation and operating performance improvement. He works "sleeves rolled up" to help companies globally achieve fundamental transformations in how they operate so they can fulfill their highest potential in the beyond digital era. He has coauthored several articles on value creation and business transformation in *Harvard Business Review* and *strategy+business*, including "Digitizing Isn't the Same as Digital Transformation," "6 Leadership Paradoxes for the Post-Pandemic Era," "The Redefined *No* of the CFO," "How to Engender a Performance Culture," and "After the Crisis: Three Actions to Reset Cost and Reshape Your Business for Growth."

Mani holds a master's degree in international public policy from Johns Hopkins University's School of Advanced International Studies and a bachelor's degree in finance and marketing from American University.